EURIPIDES' HIPPOLYTUS

Euripides' Hippolytus
Translation with Notes, Introduction and Essay

Michael R. Halleran
University of Washington

Focus Classical Library
Focus Publishing
R. Pullins Company
Newburyport MA

THE FOCUS CLASSICAL LIBRARY
Series Editors • James Clauss and Stephen Esposito

Aristophanes: Acharnians • Jeffrey Henderson
Aristophanes: The Birds • Jeffrey Henderson
Aristophanes: Clouds • Jeffrey Henderson
Aristophanes: Frogs • Henderson
Aristophanes: Lysistrata • Jeffrey Henderson
Aristophanes: Three Comedies: Acharnians, Lysistrata, Clouds • Jeffrey Henderson
Euripides: The Bacchae • Stephen Esposito
Euripides: Four Plays: Medea, Hippolytus, Heracles, Bacchae • Stephen Esposito, ed.
Euripides: Hecuba • Robin Mitchell-Boyask
Euripides: Heracles • Michael R. Halleran
Euripides: Hippolytus • Michael R. Halleran
Euripides: Medea • Anthony Podlecki
Euripides: The Trojan Women • Diskin Clay
Golden Verses: Poetry of the Augustan Age • Paul T. Alessi
Golden Prose in the Age of Augustus • Paul T. Alessi
Hesiod: Theogony • Richard Caldwell
Hesiod: Theogony & Works and Days • Stephanie Nelson
The Homeric Hymns • Susan Shelmerdine
Ovid: Metamorphoses • Z. Philip Ambrose
Plautus: Captivi, Amphitryon, Casina, Pseudolus • David Christenson
Roman Lives • Brian K. Harvey
Sophocles: Antigone • Ruby Blondell
Sophocles: Electra • Hanna M. Roisman
Sophocles: King Oidipous • Ruby Blondell
Sophocles: Oidipous at Colonus • Ruby Blondell
Sophocles: Philoktetes • Seth Schein
Sophocles: The Theban Plays • Ruby Blondell
Terence: Brothers (Adelphoe) • Charles Mercier
Vergil: The Aeneid • Richard Caldwell

To Erin, Rebecca, Tom, and Andy
with love

Table of Contents

Preface

In 1995 I published *Euripides: Hippolytus, with Introduction, Translation and Commentary* (Aris and Philips: Warminster). That book, with Greek text, English translation, and detailed commentary, was meant for a dual audience, both those with a knowledge of Greek and those without. The present work is derivative of that earlier one—and different from it in several ways.

The translation has been revised in hundreds of places. Most of the changes are slight, made in an effort to produce a more fluid rendering, while preserving, in the style of this series, the shape, images, and texture of the Greek. The use of line-end throughout is an attempt to approximate the structure of the Greek verse and should not be construed as an effort at English poetry. James Diggle, following the pathbreaking work of W. S. Barrett, published an excellent text, with full apparatus, of the play (Oxford 1984). This translation follows that text except in about a dozen places, which are discussed in my 1995 edition. Square brackets ([ ])surrounding a word, phrase or line(s) suggest that, although found in the manuscripts of this play, the bracketed text is thought by scholars to be spurious. Conversely, slanted brackets (< >) indicate that the translated words are not found in the ancient texts but are the supplements of later scholars. In a handful of places a tilde (~) suggests that the text as transmitted does not make good sense and the "translation" is makeshift. Stage directions, in the text and at times elaborated in the notes, are not found in the original manuscripts but are inferences from our knowledge of ancient stage practice.

The notes for this edition are brief and geared towards the reader coming to the play without any specialized background. They aim to supply basic information on mythological, cultural and literary issues in an effort to bridge the gaps between the worlds of fifth-century Athenians and twenty-first century Anglophone readers. Similarly, the introductory materials, modified from the earlier edition of *Hippolytus* and my edition of *Heracles* in the Focus Classical Library series, seek to locate the play in its mythological, cultural and literary contexts.

A book reaches completion only with the help of others. I begin by

ix

thanking all those who offered suggestions, advice and corrections on my 1995 *Hippolytus* commentary, and especially Chris Collard, the series editor. In developing this book for the Focus Classical Library, I benefited from the valuable suggestions of the Focus Classical Library editors, Jim Clauss and Albert Keith Whitaker. In preparing the final copy, Ron Kline and Alicia Palacio provided valuable assistance. My colleagues in the Dean's Office have created a wonderful environment in which to pursue common educational visions (and even to carry on some work in Classics). Ron Pullins, the impresario of Focus since its inception, has been a great supporter of the Classics and Classicists for many years now, and I take this opportunity to thank him for his support and friendship. Finally, and as always, my greatest thanks go happily to my wife and family. Erin Halleran read and improved the entire manuscript with her customary unerring judgment, and our children, Rebecca, Tom, and Andy, continue to complete and gladden our lives. To Erin, Rebecca, Tom, and Andy, I offer this book with admiration, gratitude and love.

MRH
University of Washington
November 2, 2000

Introduction

EURIPIDES AND HIS TIMES

Euripides' life spanned most of the fifth century BCE. He was born in the latter part of the 480s (ancient sources record both 485/4 and 480 as dates for his birth) and died in 406. He was an Athenian. His father, named Mnesarchos or Mnesarchides, and his mother Cleito were from the Attic deme Phyla. It seems that the family was reasonably well off and Euripides himself perhaps rich. He most likely received a traditional education, being schooled in letters, music and athletics. In 455 he produced his first plays, the title of one of which we know, the *Peliades* ("daughters of Pelias"). At this time Aeschylus, the most renowned playwright of the early years of the century, had just died (in 456) and Sophocles (ca. 496-406/5), was already well established as a tragic poet. Euripides did not win first prize at the festival that year and had to wait until 441 before he took that honor. In fact, Euripides, although very often awarded the honor of putting on plays at the Athenian dramatic festivals, was victorious only four times in his career, and once posthumously. He composed over ninety plays, and on occasion he also wrote in other genres. Near the end of his life he left Athens and moved to the court of Archelaos, king of Macedonia, and there he died.

In addition to the information given in the brief sketch above, ancient sources preserve many anecdotes about the poet. Many of these stories, however, are of dubious historical validity; often the plays themselves and the traditions of contemporary comedy are the source for these tidbits about the personal traits and habits of the poet. From the ancient traditions and their half-truths, however, a certain picture of the poet begins to emerge, even if the details are blurred. Euripides is said to have owned a library, and this in an age of few books. It is reported also that he had a cave on Salamis where he could avoid the crowd and that he was often lost in thought. The stories about Sophocles, themselves exaggerated and even apocryphal, suggest an ideal citizen, active in the social, religious, and military life of Athens. This picture of Sophocles and the contrasting one of Euripides were very possibly drawn in caricature in order to highlight the differences between the two men, but it seems unlikely that the differences were invented from whole cloth. The ancient sources seem to suggest that Euripides was something of a loner, who was more caught up than his contemporaries in the intellectual movements of his age.

Athens was experiencing its most exciting and stimulating era. In fact, Euripides' life is virtually framed by the rise and fall of Athenian pre-eminence. The year 480 is given as one of the dates for his birth, perhaps because of the ancient predilection for linking together important events, in this case the birth of the poet Euripides and the battle of Salamis. At this battle the Greek navy defeated the Persians, and, although hostilities between the two powers continued, this signaled an end to the threat of Persian attempts to dominate Greece. The victory not only freed Greece from the decades-old threat of Persian rule but also helped to establish the dominant role of Athens in Greek affairs, for it was the Athenian naval initiative, led by Themistocles, which drove back the Persians. What this victory over the Persians guaranteed and what the Athenians valued so dearly was freedom. Athens had recently cast off its own tyrants and was ruled by a democracy, which became even more democratic as the century progressed. There continued to be supporters of oligarchy in Athens, but they did not hold sway.

An important consequence of the prominent role of Athens in the Persian defeat was the great confidence it inspired, confidence which strengthened and characterized the city-state for most of the century. Freedom of speech was part of this confidence and of Athenian democracy. Thought of by Athenians as their privilege, this freedom helped create an environment hospitable to the great intellectual achievements of this age. In some ways Athens remained a conservative community, and trials for impiety (the most famous being that of Socrates in 399) are recorded. But Euripides, Sophocles, the comic poet Aristophanes (ca. 445- ca. 385) and others worked in a city which permitted and in no small part fostered their genius. It is difficult to imagine these dramas being written and produced in the more constricting environment of Sparta or Corinth.

In the fifty years after the defeat of the Persians, Athens would become the most powerful city-state in the Greek world and, perhaps inevitably, the most ambitious and feared. Ultimately this period of Athenian history ended when Sparta, the other leading city-state of the Greek world, and her allies went to war with Athens and her allies, in the Peloponnesian War. As the contemporary historian Thucydides wrote in his account of the war (1.23), "I consider that the truest cause [of the war], although most concealed officially, was that the Athenians, by becoming powerful and causing fear to the Spartans, compelled them to war." Hostilities had flared before between these two powers earlier in the century, but this war was on a much greater scale. With some interruptions the war went on from 431 until the defeat of Athens in 404, shortly after Euripides' death.

However short-lived Athens' dominance would prove to be, its accomplishments during this period were remarkable. Like Paris and New York in later ages, Athens was the center of artistic and intellectual activity, producing and attracting the leading practitioners of the various arts. The confidence and political leadership following the Persian Wars contributed to this in no small measure. Under Pericles, an extraordinary building program was undertaken on the acropolis, culminating in the erection of the magnificent temple to Athena, the Parthenon, which showed off Athenian excellence in architecture and sculpture. (This and other ambitious projects were aided by money collected from the so-called Delian league, which was formed originally as an alliance against the Persian threat but was eventually based in and exploited by Athens to further its empire.) Vase painting, depicting domestic and mythological scenes alike, reached its acme in this period and had its finest workshops in Athens. Athens was also the "home" for tragedy and comedy, the two most significant literary genres of the age.

Very important for Euripides' career was the contemporary intellectual movement, named after a group of men collectively referred to as the sophists. This group of men, Protagoras, Anaxagoras, and Prodicus among them, did not constitute a "school" but were individuals who toured Greece and in many instances resided in Athens for long periods. They were teachers, offering instruction in a wide variety of topics, from astronomy to rhetoric. Much of their teaching was aimed at practical knowledge which would help their students be successful at whatever they did. Rhetoric played a large role in their instruction, in part because in a democracy the ability to speak well and sway public opinion, whether in the law court or the assembly, was crucial for success. But part of their teaching was in more theoretical areas such as epistemology and theology. Some idea of the sophists' intellectual concerns may be gleaned from a few quotations. Protagoras wrote, "About the gods, I am not able to know whether they exist or not nor what form they have. For many things impede this knowledge, the obscurity [of the issue] and the shortness of a human's life" (frag. 4). And, again, "Of all things a man is the measure, of those that are, that they are, and of those that are not, that they are not" (frag. 1). These fragments give a brief glimpse of the fundamental nature of some of the sophists' inquiries. And humankind is placed at the center of the inquiry. We can also see their keen interest in rhetoric in a statement made by another sophist, Gorgias: "Speech is a great ruler, which with the smallest and least manifest body accomplishes divine deeds" (Helen 8).

Euripides is linked to these thinkers in the biographical tradition: the three men mentioned above were said to have been his teachers (the biographers' way of saying "there is a connection between"), and Socrates is recorded as his friend. Also his plays reflect the influence of these and other contemporary thinkers. Euripides was not the only playwright to be influenced by these contemporary thinkers: Sophocles and the author of Prometheus Bound, for example, also can be seen responding to the ideas and questions of these men. But Euripides, the ancient biographies reported, and his plays seem to reveal, was more influenced by them. Or perhaps it is more accurate to say that he was more concerned with the issues with which they too were concerned. Rhetoric, at times self-conscious, is more prominent in his plays than in those of Aeschylus and Sophocles. And questions of the gods and divine justice are at the forefront of several of his plays, as we see, for example, in Hippolytus, Heracles, and Bacchae. Stories of Euripides being charged with impiety may well be apocryphal, but they reflect the discomfort which some Athenians may have felt at his frequently disturbing plays.

Although only mildly successful in his own time, Euripides' works became very popular after his death, in part because his interests prefigured those of later ages. (In fact, Euripides is often thought of as the most modern of the three tragedians.) His plays were frequently performed and their texts often reproduced. Owing to his later popularity and a stroke of good fortune, many more plays of Euripides survive than of Sophocles or Aeschylus. Eighteen genuine plays (plus the probably spurious Rhesus) are found in the manuscripts. We have, in other words, almost a full fifth of the poet's total dramatic output, compared with, for example, about six percent of Sophocles' plays. In addition to these plays which are preserved in full, many fragments from other plays survive (more than in the case of the other two tragedians). Often of considerable size, these fragments, in conjunction with ancient plot summaries and other information, allow for a reconstruction of the plays. In short, we have a fuller picture of Euripides' dramatic work than we have for either Aeschylus or Sophocles.

The fuller picture provided by the greater number of extant plays does not permit a monolithic view of the playwright. Several of his plays, for example, often called the "romances" (Helen, Ion, and the Iphigenia among the Taurians) have "happy endings" and do not conform to a strict notion of tragedy. Other plays have unusual structures and twists, while others offer very novel treatment of the mythological material. The many Euripidean plays that survive suggest a complex, clever and thoughtful playwright. And we should be careful not to isolate the "intellectual" side of his dramas, as if it could be divorced from the plays themselves: Euripides was a dramatist, writing plays that were meant to be performed and most fully understood in performance.

THE *HIPPOLYTUS* IN PERFORMANCE

The *Hippolytus* was first performed in 428 BCE in Athens at an annual religious festival. The day it was performed, some 15,000 people, mainly Athenians, gathered together in the large, open-air theater of Dionysus, which was located in the god's precinct and adjacent to his temple on the southeastern slope of the acropolis, to view the plays to be presented that day. The *Hippolytus* was a play called a *tragoidia*, a tragedy, or more generally a *drama*. *Drama* etymologically means "the thing done, enacted." Yet our direct experience is with the written word, and even this is tenuous, as the earliest manuscript which preserves this play dates from the eleventh century. Moreover the play in this (and other) manuscripts is removed from its context, and it offers no explicit stage directions or information about the music and dance that were part of the performance. The words themselves are vivid, moving, and finely textured poetry, but we must remember that they were part of a larger structure of words and action. Fortunately, the plays themselves, while containing no explicit information about production, provide much evidence from which to make inferences and to establish the patterns and conventions of the ancient Greek theater. There are also two other rich sources of information: writers in later antiquity provided anecdotes and material which can be mined and sifted for useful gems, and the archaeological record, including, of course, the remains of the theaters themselves, tells us a great deal about the physical circumstances of performance.

The theater of Dionysus was large. At the time of Lycurgus (latter part of the fourth century BCE) it could seat by modern estimates approximately 15,000 spectators. Built on the southeastern slope of the acropolis, its rows of seats went up the hill. The viewing area was called the *theatron*, whence English "theater;" the performance itself took place below. The *orchestra*, a spacious circular dancing area, dominated the spectator's view. About sixty-five feet in diameter, it was the chief area of activity during the play. The other main focus of attention was the *skene*, an (originally) wooden building, with a roof strong enough to support more than one actor, located at the far side of the *orchestra*. It served as the backdrop for the play's action, being the palace at Trozen in *Hippolytus*, or whatever the world of the play claimed. Some scene painting was employed, but our knowledge of this aspect of the original productions is meager. In addition to providing the backdrop for the drama's action, the *skene* also was a stage building, a changing room. The building also helped in projecting the actors' voices in the large open-air theater. The *skene* had one central double door, and it very possibly also had one or two side doors in this period. Certainly some scenes in some plays would have been much easier to stage if we assume more than one door was available for comings and goings.

The *skene* offered one place from which characters in the play could enter and to which they could exit. But characters could also enter into the *orchestra* and leave it along the two long entrance ramps, each one called an *eisodos* (often called today, less accurately, *parodos*), which led at angles on either side into the acting area. Most of the entrances and exits in a Greek tragedy occurred along these long ramps. It is important to remember in this regard the great openness of the Greek theater: "The dramatic weight of comings and goings is proportional to the openness of space that the Greek theater presented to the playwright, who was also the producer, for exploitation."[1]

Characters in the dramas usually entered and exited on the ground, but could also appear on high. A crane-like device called the *mechane* was available for divine appearances aloft. The roof of the skene could also be used for divine appearances as well as for mortals' activities. The *ekkyklema* is another device whose existence, although certain for later periods in the theater, is doubted by some for the fifth century. The *ekkyklema* was a platform that could be rolled out into the acting area, permitting an interior scene to be shown to the audience. One of the conventions of the Greek stage was that all the action takes place outdoors, so anything that occurs inside must be revealed to the audience through voices from offstage, an eye-witness account of the event, or the scene presented on the *ekkyklema*.

The existence of a raised stage at this point in the history of the theater is uncertain. Later in the history of the theater the stage became significantly elevated, furthering the distance and distinction between the world of the chorus and the world of the actors. This was not the case in the fifth century. As the plays themselves make amply clear, even if the actors are on a slightly raised platform, they and the

[1]   J. Gould, "Tragedy in Performance," in *The Cambridge History of Classical Literature*, vol. 1 *Greek Literature*, ed. P. Easterling and B. Knox (Cambridge 1985) 270.

chorus communicate freely with one another and can impinge on each other's acting area; no barrier is felt between the two groups. On balance it seems as if there was a slightly elevated platform extending from the *skene* used by the actors, while the chorus, the other members of the production, operated in the *orchestra* proper.

Tragedy was very much a part of the *polis*, the city-state, and had been since the performance of tragedies was first instituted by the *polis* in ca. 534. The plays were put on during a religious festival, the City Dionysia, sponsored by the state in honor of the god Dionysus, and were financially supported by wealthy citizens chosen by a state official. (The tragedians had other opportunities for producing their plays, but the original forum for their productions, the City Dionysia, remained the most prestigious and consistently drew, it seems, the best dramatists.) As the occasion was a religious holiday, work was suspended and a relatively large number of the citizens would attend. The holiday was an annual festival celebrated over several days in the month Elaphebolion (roughly late March by our calendar). The festival included a torchlight procession, sacrifice, and various artistic competitions (choruses, tragedies and comedies). Although these plays were performed at a religious festival, they were not religious in the sense in which we usually understand the term: they were not necessarily or even frequently about religious dogma or ritual. Although, like so much of Greek literature, they often were in part concerned with questions of the gods' interaction with mortals, these plays honored the gods primarily by their excellence, their display of artistic achievement.

Greek society was agonistic. The plays were put on in competition: three playwrights competed for prizes. Even to be able to compete one had to be selected by the official in charge of the festival, the eponymous archon (the magistrate who gave his name to the Athenian calendar year), who presumably made his selection on the basis of a sample of the playwright's work. In the expression of the Greeks, a playwright, wishing to put on plays at the festival, "asked for a chorus" and the archon "granted a chorus." Each of the three playwrights would produce three tragedies and a satyr play, a type of burlesque (of which Euripides' *Cyclops* is the only extant example). The same magistrate who selected the three poets to put on plays at the festival also chose three of the city's wealthy citizens to finance most of the expenses incurred in a production. The *choregos,* as each of these three men was called, although he could influence a production's outcome considerably by his generosity or parsimony, was not in charge of the nuts and bolts of production. These duties fell to the playwright, who was director, usually choreographer, and, originally, though later only occasionally, actor for the plays.

Two groups comprised the performers of a Greek tragedy: actors and chorus. All the participants seem to have worn the same basic outfit: an ankle-length robe or tunic *(chiton)* with an outer garment *(himation)* over it. Footwear in this period was not elaborate but consisted of a simple thin-soled shoe or boot; occasionally actors or chorus would appear barefoot. Of course there would be variations in costume within a given production and differences from one production to another. All parts were played by men (compare the *onnagata* roles in Japan's Kabuki theater). This might tax our response as spectators, but for the original audience the playing of female roles by male actors both was conventional and was aided greatly by an important feature of these performances—the wearing of masks. The actors, as well as the members of the chorus, all wore full-face masks. Made in this period probably of reinforced linen, they covered the front of the head and had wigs attached. Although no mask survives from this era, vase painting and the evidence of the plays themselves suggest that in general an attempt was made at realism. (Writing in the second century CE, Pollux lists twenty-eight different types of mask, but the situation in Euripides' day is not certain.) The basic requirement of the mask was to identify a character in distinction from the other characters in the drama. The use of masks not only allowed this recognition of characters (the old man, the young woman, etc.), it also encouraged a close identification between the actor and the role. And, of course, the mask did not permit changes in facial expression, the type of nuance which we, accustomed to close-up shots in cinema, have come to expect. (Such fine touches in any case would have been lost to the great majority of spectators in the vast theater of Dionysus.) The mask with its unchanging expression drew attention, as one critic has put it, "not to the unexpressed thought inside, but to the distant, heroic figures, whose constant ethos it portrays."[2]

Of the two constituent parts of a Greek tragedy the chorus perhaps seems the more distant and difficult for a modern audience to appreciate. The members of the chorus, fifteen in number when the *Hippolytus* was produced, acted usually as a group, singing and dancing their part, a continuous presence in the *orchestra* once they entered. (Their number included a chorus leader, *coryphaeus*, who would at times act independently of the larger group.) This is not what we are used to in modern drama. Music and dance were integral features of the choral elements of the drama. (In fact the Greek word *choros*

---

[2]   O. Taplin, *Greek Tragedy in Action* (Berkeley and Los Angeles 1978) 14.

has "dance" as its primary meaning.) Music from a reed instrument, the *aulos*, accompanied the performance of the dancing, but the precise nature of the music and of the dancing is impossible to determine from the ancient evidence, although we do know that in general Greek dancing was mimetic.

Even with little information about the music and dance, it is readily apparent that the choral lyrics are rich poetry and important to the drama. All parts of a Greek drama, both the dialogue and the songs, were composed in verse, but the poetry of the songs was different in kind: denser, more striking in its imagery and more suggestive in its language. The chorus has over the years been called the "ideal spectator" and the "voice of the poet." Neither is true. Although the chorus is generally less well defined and at times less integral to the action than the other characters in the play, it does have a specific personality (in our play the women of Trozen) and a definite role to play in the drama. The chorus responds to the action, reflecting on the events and often referring to past events as a context for the current ones. Owing to the nature of their poetry and their function, the choral songs are heard in, as it were, a different key. The typical choral song is strophic, that is to say it is written in paired stanzas, each member of the pair having the same metrical composition. The first member is called the *strophe* and the second the *antistrophe*. While the two members of the pair of stanzas are identical rhythmically, no two pairs are alike. After one, two, three or even more paired stanzas, the ode may conclude with a single stanza with no responding element; this is called an epode. The first song is called the *parodos*, the song usually delivered as the chorus entered into the *orchestra*; subsequent ones are each called a *stasimon*, a song delivered after the chorus had taken up their position in the *orchestra*.

Our traditions about Greek tragedy point to an origin in a song sung at a ritual. The name Thespis is attached to the first actor, and this man is often called the creator of tragedy: at a time of thoroughly choral presentations, he is said to be the first to break away from the chorus and give speeches and respond to the chorus. With this major innovation, tragedy ceased to be only a sung narrative and became enriched with a new dimension, that of actors and their *spoken* words. After the introduction of the first actor, others were later added: Aeschylus is said to have introduced the second actor and Sophocles the third. There the number of actors with speaking parts became fixed: each dramatist worked with only three actors. Of course a play could have more than three characters, but this would be handled by the "doubling" of roles: one actor would play more than one part. There were so-called "mute characters," "extras" who would have silent parts to play, such as attendants and children. The reason for this limit was perhaps aesthetic, or maybe it reflects an attempt at fairness so that all playwrights would be competing for the prizes under the same conditions. Whatever the reason, the effect is note-worthy: the Greek tragic stage, with the exception of the chorus, tended to be rather uncrowded. Dialogue among three characters, although possible, was in fact uncommon. The plays generally show conversa-tions between two characters, or one character and the chorus, or one delivering a soliloquy. Even when the three actors with speaking parts are on stage together, they only infrequently carry on a three-way dialogue. The doubling of roles necessitated by the relatively small number of actors was also facilitated by the masks and the identifica-tion they created between the mask-wearing actor and the character he played. In a given drama an actor might play several roles, and with each mask that he donned he became that character and the au-dience could thereby readily make the adjustment.

As Aristotle long ago observed, the fundamental structure of tragedy is based on the alternation of speech and song, the dialogue of the actors and the songs of the chorus. Periodically in the play the chorus leader will have a few lines to speak, and the actors will occa-sionally sing their lines, but the basic dynamic of the genre is the al-ternation of speech and song. This alternation gives tragedy much of its rich and varied texture. Tragedy's structure also involves not only the alternation of speech and song but this alternation tied up with exits before the song and entrances after them. One should be alert to this basic pattern and variations on it.

HIPPOLYTUS IN MYTH AND CULT

The basic story pattern is an old and common one: a young man becomes the object of a married woman's desire, rebuffs her sexual overtures, and is then falsely accused to the woman's husband of rape. With variations, Greek mythology told this tale about Bellerophon and Stheneboea, Phoenix and his father's concubine, and Peleus and Astydamia, and versions of it are found in many cultures.[3] This com-mon mythological pattern developed also around Hippolytus and Phaedra, only in this case the situation is further complicated by the woman being the wife of the young man's father, Theseus. Although in some form the story with these three figures may stem from the

---

[3] This common motif is often named after Potiphar's wife from the version of the story in *Genesis* 39. In general see S. Thompson, *Motif-Index of Folk-Literature*, rev. ed. (Bloomington 1955-8), 4.474-5 ("Potiphar's Wife") and 5.386, ("Lustful Stepmother").

archaic period (or beyond), it does not come into prominence until given shape by fifth-century tragedy.

Hippolytus leaves little trace of any sort before the fifth century. His very name is elusive. It suggests something about horses and loosing, and *may* very well refer to the circumstances of his death—"loosed by horses." The ancient mythographer Apollodorus (3.10.3) reports that in the epic *Naupactia* (composed perhaps in the sixth century) Asclepius raises him from the dead, a story which Pindar tells allusively (*Pyth.* 3.54ff.). He does not appear in Greek art until the following century, the earliest representations being on Italian vases showing his death by his horses.

Hippolytus was also the object of cult worship, both in Athens and especially in Trozen, and this latter cult likely goes back to the Bronze Age. At the end of this play, Artemis establishes a cult, as Euripidean gods often do in the play's conclusion, in honor of Hippolytus, in which young Trozenian women will offer him locks of their hair before their weddings. The cult to which she refers was active at least through the second century CE, when the traveler Pausanias (2.32.1) reports this cult practice. Pausanias also implies the great antiquity of the cult in recording that it was established by Diomedes, a figure imagined to be from the late Bronze Age. In the same passage (2.32.3) we also learn that in the same enclosed area the Trozenians had a stadium named in Hippolytus' honor above which stood a temple of Aphrodite *Kataskopia* (the "Spy"), so named because from there Phaedra would gaze at her beloved exercising. Nearby was a statue of the god Asclepius (2.32.4), who in various accounts of the myth was responsible for resurrecting Hippolytus.

Just as Artemis at the end of the play refers to the cult of Hippolytus in Trozen, Aphrodite at the beginning alludes to the cult of Hippolytus in Athens. The goddess explains that Phaedra, stricken with passion for her stepson, established on the acropolis a temple to Aphrodite to be named later "in memory of Hippolytus" (32). Inscriptions dated (coincidentally?) to the time of or a few years after the production of this play link the veneration of Aphrodite to that of Hippolytus on the south slope of the acropolis. While we know next to nothing about this shrine to Hippolytus, it clearly was associated with Aphrodite, and it stood near the sanctuary of Asclepius (Pausanias 1.22.1). Thus in both Trozen and Athens, these two are linked in worship and associated, if only tangentially, with Asclepius.

The only mention of Phaedra before the fifth century occurs in the *Nekuia* of Homer's *Odyssey* (11.321), where she is named, along with Procris and Ariadne, among the women in the underworld. The association with Procris, the daughter of the Athenian king Erectheus, and the Cretan Ariadne, who is commonly represented as Phaedra's sister, indicates a presumed association with both Athens and Crete. Phaedra is the daughter of Minos and Pasiphaë and much is made in the play of her Cretan past. Because, according to most accounts, Minos refused to sacrifice a certain bull to Poseidon, the god took vengeance by making his wife enamored of the bull.[4] Assisted by the disguise of a wooden cow fashioned by Daedalus, Pasiphaë satisfied her desire and produced a hybrid bull-child, the Minotaur (cf. *Hipp*. 337-8). When Theseus came to Crete in order to stop the Athenian tribute of young men and women to the Minotaur, he was aided by Ariadne, who had fallen in love with him. About what happened after Theseus killed the Minotaur our sources differ: at some point Dionysus becomes Ariadne's husband and in some accounts (see esp. *Od*. 11.324-5) this ends unhappily (cf. *Hipp*. 339). Phaedra has virtually no mythology apart from her Cretan associations and the tale linking her with Hippolytus; the circumstances leading up to her wedding to Theseus are not known.

By the sixth century Theseus became the major figure in Athenian mythology, a character modeled on the great pan-Hellenic hero Heracles. He had close associations with both Athens and Trozen. Like many heroes (Heracles being the most notable example), Theseus had a mortal and an immortal father, his mortal father Aegeus being king of Athens, his immortal father Poseidon worshipped as king in Trozen. His mother, Aethra, was Trozenian, and an essential part of the Theseus legend was his journey from Trozen to Athens to be accepted by Aegeus, during which he encountered and dispatched many villains. His adventure with the Amazons is confusing in many details, but clear in linking him amorously with one of the Amazons, whom he abducts in most, especially early, versions of the tale. This woman's name is most commonly (and on sixth-century vases exclusively) Antiope, and she becomes the mother of Hippolytus. In *Hippolytus*, she is simply referred to as "the Amazon," and great stress is laid on Hippolytus' bastard status.[5] Accounts of how her liaison with Theseus

---

4   Bulls play a prominent role in the mythology relevant to the Hippolytus story. Minos is the child of Europa and Zeus in the form of a bull; Poseidon has a special association with bulls, as seen here and in his sending a bull against Hippolytus' horses; Pasiphaë, too, has an obvious involvement with bulls; Theseus, in addition to slaying the Minotaur, also, shortly after his arrival in Athens, captures the dangerous bull of Marathon.

5   It is possible that in versions prior to this play, Hippolytus was in fact the legitimate offspring of Theseus and Antiope. The issue of legitimacy would resonate deeply among the Athenians, who in 451/0 had

ended vary (most commonly she is killed in battle either against or on the side of Theseus), and sometime after this union, Theseus marries Phaedra and has children by her.

When *Hippolytus*, the earliest extant full treatment of this story, opens, the ingredients for the tragedy are already in place. As Aphrodite herself explains in the prologue, she has taken action to ensure Hippolytus' punishment for willfully neglecting her. When Hippolytus came from Trozen to Athens to participate in the Mysteries, Phaedra, because of Aphrodite's power, fell in love. Later, exiled from Athens for killing his cousins, the Pallantids, Theseus took up residence with Phaedra in Trozen. When the play opens, Theseus is out of the country, and Phaedra, unwilling to yield to an overpowering desire for her stepson, has already determined, as we learn later, to die by starvation. Phaedra's Nurse determines the cause of Phaedra's malady and with this information approaches Hippolytus. The young man is shocked at the Nurse's proposition of a sexual encounter with his stepmother and leaves the stage, promising to return. Phaedra, fearing that Hippolytus will damage her good reputation by reporting the Nurse's proposition as her own, writes a letter falsely accusing Hippolytus of rape, and takes her own life. When Theseus returns to discover his wife's corpse and letter, he exiles and curses his son. This curse proves effective, as Poseidon grants his wish that Hippolytus be killed, by sending a terrifying bull from the sea. Hippolytus' horses, overcome with fear, bring about their master's death. Finally, with the appearance of Artemis, Theseus learns the truth about what really happened.

In watching this play in 428 BCE, spectators at the City Dionysia in Athens witnessed a remarkable event: Euripides' *Hippolytus* was the *second* treatment the playwright had given to the myth, the only certain instance of an Athenian tragedian rewriting a play.[6] Earlier he had produced a different play on this topic, a play which was a failure, while *Hippolytus* and the other plays produced by Euripides in 428 were awarded first prize in the dramatic competition. What do we know about that earlier play?

---

passed a highly restrictive citizenship law, limiting full rights to those with *two* citizen parents.

[6] While we do not know *for certain* that the extant play is the later of the two, with almost all scholars, I accept this relative dating and refer to the two plays as *Hippolytus I* (the first one) and simply *Hippolytus* (the extant play).

THE FIRST *HIPPOLYTUS*

Writing in the late third or early second century BCE, Aristophanes of Byzantium explained that the surviving play must have been second because it "corrected" what was "unseemly and worthy of condemnation" in the first. About that first play, at times called *Hippolytos (Kata)kaluptomenos* ("*Hippolytus Veiled*"), we have some twenty (short) fragments and a few late sources that *might* inform us about the first play. What Aristophanes of Byzantium meant by "corrected" is probably indicated in an ancient *Life* of Euripides and the comic playwright Aristophanes' *Frogs* (1043, 1052-4), which both suggest a Phaedra intent upon adultery. Such a Phaedra must come from *Hippolytus I* and would conform to the mythological stereotype of "Potiphar's wife" (see above, p. xx-xxi) and contrast sharply with the virtuous and discreet Phaedra of *Hippolytus*. In the following sketch of *Hippolytus I* I offer what I think of as a reasonably likely account of the first play. Much, however, remains unknown or uncertain.[7]

Like all extant Euripidean plays, *Hippolytus I* began with an expository prologue, which was spoken by Phaedra. We now know that the play was very likely set in Trozen, which would have been clearly indicated in this opening speech. Phaedra's Nurse, a staple of the story, must have been a character in this play, even though she left no definite traces in the fragments. We can say very little about the chorus, who would have entered after the opening scene, except that, like the chorus in *Hippolytus*, they were female and probably Trozenian. Either in the prologue scene, or in the first episode, Phaedra and the Nurse had a scene in which they discuss Phaedra's passion. Several of the surviving fragments seem to come from this scene. Certainly, in typical Euripidean (and Sophoclean) fashion, Hippolytus was depicted in a scene before his encounter with Phaedra. A line giving advice not to be unbending in chastity *might* come from that scene, which *may* have included a servant (or comrade) of Hippolytus. A direct confrontation between Phaedra and Hippolytus is assumed universally, and suggested by a number of the fragments. In this confrontation, Phaedra would have most likely tried to seduce Hippolytus with the lure of Theseus' throne. An oath from Hippolytus was probably secured in this scene, as a line referring to the consequences of violating a supplication seems to indicate.

The distinguishing epithet sometimes given to the title of the first play *(Kata)kaluptomenos*, very plausibly stems from a scene in which the shocked Hippolytus covered himself with his cloak in response to

---

[7]   A fuller account of these fragments and the reconstruction of the first *Hippolytus* can be found in my 1995 commentary.

Phaedra's overtures. (For self-veiling on stage in shame and fear, cf. *Hipp.* 243ff.) At some point thereafter (the following scene?) Phaedra in some way falsely accused Hippolytus to Theseus, who has been conveniently out of the picture. How the false allegation of rape was made (Phaedra directly? by falsified evidence?) is unclear, but it obviously must occur before the confrontation between Theseus and Hippolytus. Like most Euripidean plays (including *Hippolytus*), this play probably had an *agon* between Theseus and Hippolytus, and several fragments, including one lamenting clever rhetoric, suggest it. At some point Theseus must pronounce his curse against Hippolytus (it was a fixture of the myth); I posit that it was hurled *after* the *agon*. Hippolytus might have also been banished with exile, but his departure could equally be an (understandable) response to his father's curse.

There can be no doubt that this play had a messenger scene describing Hippolytus' disastrous chariot ride, and one fragment comes from that speech. The fragments are completely silent about Phaedra's suicide, which most probably occurred *after* Hippolytus' death. (Hippolytus' death would itself have happened off-stage; the scene in the second play of his final pain-wracked moments and his reconciliation with his father seems very much unique to it.) Perhaps Phaedra responds to the news of Hippolytus' death with (an off-stage) suicide, which could then have been reported by the Nurse. It is improbable that Phaedra reveals the truth to Theseus; the Nurse or the divinity appearing at the end of the play most likely performed this function. The last part of the play would be very pressed if upon the debate between father and son, there followed a) a report of Hippolytus' death, b) Phaedra's revelation of the truth to Theseus, c) a report of her death, and d) appearance of a divinity. The play concluded with a divine appearance. The four-line choral tag that survives, referring to Hippolytus' future cult, allows one to infer that the play conformed to many other Euripidean dramas in having a divinity who appeared on high and who, among other things, predicted Hippolytus' future cult. The most likely candidate for this role is Artemis, Hippolytus' patron. Since the play was *not* set in Athens, Aphrodite's connection to Hippolytus' cult there makes her irrelevant in this context; Poseidon, Theseus' father and responsible for fulfilling Theseus' curse, is a (less likely) possibility.

Hippolytus

APHRODITE
HIPPOLYTUS
ATTENDANTS OF HIPPOLYTUS
SERVANT
CHORUS OF TROZENIAN WOMEN
NURSE
PHAEDRA
THESEUS
MESSENGER
ARTEMIS

Aphrodite enters from one of the eisodoi.

Aphrodite
    I am powerful and not without a name among mortals
    and within the heavens. I am called the goddess Cypris.

Setting: The play is set in Trozen, with the *skene* building representing the palace. Statues of Aphrodite and Artemis stand on opposite sides of the acting area.

Aphrodite enters: Euripides always opened his plays with an expository speech laying out the drama's background. When a divine character delivers the prologue, as is the case here, the references to the future create an irony in which the audience knows what awaits the play's mortals characters but the latter do not. Aphrodite may have appeared on the roof of the skene building or at ground level. In either case, like the other divine characters who deliver the prologues in Euripides' plays, she makes no direct contact with the mortal characters and departs before Hippolytus arrives.

1: **powerful:** Aphrodite's power is announced at the very outset, the first word in the Greek text.

2: **Cypris:** A common name, especially in poetry, for Aphrodite, reflecting her association with the island of Cyprus.

1

Of those who dwell within Pontus
and the boundaries of Atlas and see the light of the sun,
I treat well those who revere my power,   5
but I trip up those who are proud towards me.
For this principle holds among the race of the gods also:
they enjoy being honored by mortals.
I shall now show you the truth of these words:
Theseus' son, Hippolytus, the Amazon's offspring,   10
reared by pure Pittheus—
he alone of the citizens of this land of Trozen
says that I am by nature the most vile of divinities.
He spurns the bed and doesn't touch marriage,
but honors Apollo's sister, Artemis,   15
the daughter of Zeus, considering her the greatest of divinities.
Always consorting with the virgin through the green wood,
he rids the land of beasts with swift dogs,
having come upon a more than mortal companionship.
I don't begrudge them these things; why should I?   20
But I will punish Hippolytus this day
for the wrongs he has done me. I won't need much toil,
since long before this I prepared most of what has to be done.
     When he once came from Pittheus' house
to the land of Pandion for viewing the rites
at the holy Mysteries, his father's noble wife   25

3-4: **Pontus . . . boundaries of Atlas**: the Black Sea and Straits of Gibraltar respectively, that is, from the ancient Greeks' perspective the eastern and western limits of the known world.

10: **Amazon's offspring**: nowhere in the play is Hippolytus' mother named. What is emphasized consistently is that he is a bastard, the illegitimate offspring of Theseus and the (non-Greek) Amazon.

11: **Pittheus**: Hippolytus' paternal great-grandfather; his daughter Aethra was Theseus' mother.

14: Remarkably what Aphrodite demands from Hippolytus is not simply ritual observance, but his participation in her realm, the world of sex and marriage.

17: **consorting**: The word, often used in a sexual sense, suggests the unnaturalness (from Aphrodite's viewpoint) of this association.

24: **land of Pandion**: Athens, as Pandion was one of the city's legendary kings.

25: **Mysteries**: These were the rites celebrated at Eleusis, outside of Athens, in honor of the goddess Demeter. This detail suggests Hippolytus' religious piety while offering a plausible motive for his visit to Athens.

Phaedra looked at him and her heart was seized
with a terrible passion, according to my plans.
And before coming to this land of Trozen
she set up there a temple to Cypris
beside Pallas' very rock,   30
overlooking this land, since she was in love with
one who was distant. In the future people will name the goddess
as established there because of Hippolytus.
After that, to escape the pollution of the Pallantids' blood,
Theseus left the land of Cecrops   35
and, resigned to a year in exile,
sailed with his wife to this land.
And now the poor woman, moaning and overwhelmed
by the goads of passion, is dying
in silence—none of the household knows her disease.   40
     But not like this is this love destined to turn out;
I will reveal the matter to Theseus and it will be brought to light.
As for the young man who wars against me,
his father will kill him with the curses the lord of the sea,
Poseidon, gave to Theseus as a gift,   45
that he could pray to the god three times not in vain.
Phaedra will keep her good reputation,
     but still she will die. For I do not value her suffering more

---

29-33: An ancient inscription links the temple of Aphrodite with the shrine of
     Hippolytus; see Introduction, p. xxi.
30: **Pallas' very rock**: the Athenian acropolis; Pallas is another name for Athena.
34: **Pallantids' blood**: The Pallantids ("sons of Pallas") were Theseus' cous-
     ins (sons of Aegeus' half-brother Pallas, not to be confused with the
     alternate name for Athena). In a dispute over his right to rule after his
     father's death, Theseus killed his cousins and went into exile for a year as
     atonement for shedding kindred blood.
35: **land of Cecrops**: Cecrops was a legendary king of Athens. Greek poetry
     used many such periphrases for common names like Athens.
40: **in silence**: Enjambed to appear at the end of its clause and the first word
     in this line, silence is highlighted at this early stage of the drama. Speech
     and silence form an intricate leitmotif in this play. See Essay, p. 68-9.
42: Not quite. The order of events—revelation, Hippolytus' death, and
     Phaedra's death—is the opposite of what transpires. While Theseus *even-
     tually* learns the truth, this line creates a false expectation of how events
     will unfold.
48: **good reputation**: This is the overriding motivation for her actions—
     her good name. See Essay, p. 69-71.

than my enemy's paying me
such a penalty that I am satisfied.   50
   But I see Theseus' son coming here,
Hippolytus, who has just abandoned the toil of the hunt;
I will depart from this place.
A band of many lively attendants follows him
and shouts with him, honoring the goddess Artemis   55
in hymns. He does not know that the gates of Hades
lie open and that this is the last light he sees.

Aphrodite exits by the same eisodos *she entered from.*

Hippolytus and his attendants enter from the opposite eisodos.

Hippolytus
Follow me, follow, hymning
the child of Zeus, heavenly Artemis, who cares for us.   60
Hippolytus and Attendants
Lady, lady, most revered,
offspring of Zeus,
hail, I say, hail, daughter
of Leto and Zeus, Artemis,   65
most beautiful by far of maidens,
you who in the expanse of heaven
dwell in the hall of your great father,
in the gold-rich house of Zeus.
Hail, I say, most beautiful,   70
most beautiful of those on Olympus.
Hippolytus
For you, mistress, I bring this plaited wreath.
I fashioned it from an untouched meadow,
where neither the shepherd thinks it right to feed his flocks 75
nor the scythe has yet come, but a bee

61-71: This brief song employs the language commonly found in hymns: frequent address, repetitions, and references to the god's attributes, parentage, dwellings and sites of worship.

73-87: Hippolytus addresses the statue of Artemis on stage and offers it the garland he has fashioned from his special meadow. The language is particularly charged, juxtaposing images of religious observance and purity with suggestions of sexual violation, since a meadow was a proverbial site for sexual activity.

goes through the untouched meadow in springtime.
And Reverence cultivates it with river water
for those to whom nothing is taught, but in whose nature
moderation has been allotted in everything always—   80
for these to cull; but for the wicked it is not right.
So, dear mistress, receive from a reverent hand
a band for your golden hair.
For I alone of mortals have this privilege:
I am your companion and converse with you,   85
hearing your voice, though without seeing your face.
May I reach the end of my life's course just as I began it!

A servant enters from the palace.

Servant
Lord—for we must call the gods masters—
would you take some good advice from me?

Hippolytus
Yes, indeed. Otherwise I wouldn't seem wise.   90

Servant
Now, do you know the law that is established among mortals?

Hippolytus
I don't know. *What* are you asking me about?

78: **Reverence**: The Greek word *aidos* is difficult to translate. It refers to a
     complex set of emotions, most particularly those that inhibit one from
     improper behavior. See Essay, p. 70.
79-80: Hippolytus wants to restrict his meadow not only to the pure but
     those who are so *by nature*. The late fifth century was engaged in a lively
     debate over nature and nurture. Throughout the play, Hippolytus em-
     phasizes his *natural* qualities and virtues. On the exclusivity of Hippolytus'
     worship, see below, p. 84-5.
80: **moderation**: No concept is more fundamental to this play than *sophrosyne*;
     which relates especially to Hippolytus and Phaedra, both of whom use
     the word in a range of senses. See Essay, p. 71-2.
86: **without seeing your face**: Hippolytus' close relationship to Artemis has
     limits—he never sees her; see below, 1391-2.
88-120: The servant serves a large function in a small scene—a foil for both
     Hippolytus' rash actions as well as Aphrodite's. The dialogue, highlighted
     by the rapid exchange of single lines (*stichomythia*) is finely nuanced, as
     the servant tries to steer Hippolytus to a safer course.

Servant
To hate what's proud and not friendly to all.

Hippolytus
Rightly—for what mortal who is proud is not irksome?

Servant
And there is some charm in being affable?   95

Hippolytus
Very much so, and profit with little effort.

Servant
Do you suppose that this same thing holds among the gods too?

Hippolytus
Yes, if we mortals follow the same laws as the gods.

Servant
Why then don't you address a proud goddess?

Hippolytus
Whom? Be careful that your tongue doesn't slip in some way.   100

Servant
This one, who stands near your gates.

Hippolytus
Since I am pure, I greet this one from afar.

Servant
And yet she is proud and renowned among mortals.   103

Hippolytus
I like none of the gods who are worshipped at night.   106

Servant
One must, child, engage in the honors due the gods.   107

Hippolytus
Among both gods and mortals one cares for one,
another for another.   104

Servant
May you be fortunate, having all the sense you need.   105

Hippolytus
Go, attendants, enter the house
and take care of the meal; after hunting a full table

93: **proud**: The word *semnos*, appearing 4x in this dialogue, covers both negative ("arrogant," "proud") and positive ("august," "revered") senses. Its
multivalence allows the servant to suggest subtly that Hippolytus'
"proud" behavior might offend a "proud" goddess.

is a pleasurable thing. And we must curry   110
the horses, so that, after I have sated myself with food,
I may yoke them to the chariot and give them their proper exercise.
But to that Cypris of yours I say good riddance.

Hippolytus and his attendants exit into the palace.

Servant
The young when they think that way
should not be imitated. But I, as is fitting for slaves to speak,   115
will pray to your statue,
mistress Cypris; and you should be forgiving.
If someone because of his youth has an intense spirit
and speaks rashly about you, pretend not to hear him;
for gods ought to be wiser than mortals.   120

The servant exits into the palace.

The chorus, fifteen women of Trozen, enter from one of the eisodoi, *likely
the same one used by Hippolytus and his attendants.*

Chorus
Strophe A
There is a rock which, they say, drips water from Oceanus,
and it pours forth from its cliffs
a flowing stream, where pitchers are dipped.
There a friend of mine   125
was soaking purple
robes in the stream's water

113: **of yours . . . I say good riddance**: Both phrases suggest Hippolytus'
    contempt. The latter is weaker than "go to hell" but probably stronger
    than the now somewhat quaint "good riddance."
114: Like Pentheus in the *Bacchae*, Hippolytus is characterized by his youth.
    See, e.g., Aphrodite's description at 43.
120: The gods, suggests the servant, should be wiser than mortals. This pithy
    axiom lingers in counterpoint to the play's actions.
121ff. Women of Trozen constitute the chorus. By virtue of their sex, they will
    be sympathetic to Phaedra. In their opening song, commonly called the
    parodos, they express their concern for and ignorance about Phaedra's
    condition. After the religious discourse of the prologue, their opening
    domestic scene stands in sharp contrast—something both mundane and
    particularly female. Formally the song has two strophic pairs (strophe
    and antistrophe) and a concluding stanza (epode).
121: **Oceanus**: The fresh-water river that the Greeks believed circled the (flat)
    earth.

and laying them down on the back of a hot,
sun-struck rock; it was from there
that word of my mistress first came to me: 130

Antistrophe A
that she wastes away in bed with a sickness, and keeps
   herself within
the house, and delicate robes
shadow her blond head.
And I hear that today is the third   135
day that she has kept
her body pure of Demeter's grain
by starvation,
wishing to run ashore on the wretched boundary
of death because of a secret trouble.   140

Strophe B
Are you frenzied, girl,
possessed by Pan or Hecate,
or the holy Corybantes
or the mountain mother?
Or are you wasting away   145
because of offenses against Dictynna of many animals,
because you neglected to make ritual offerings?
For she roams also through the Mere
and over the sandbar
in the wet whirlpools of the brine.   150

Antistrophe B
Or does someone in the house
tend to your husband,

131: **sickness**: Throughout the play, Phaedra's passion for Hippolytus and her response to it are described as a sickness.

137: **Demeter's grain**: Demeter was the Greeks' goddess of grain.

141-4: The chorus speculate that Phaedra's illness might be caused by divine possession, either of **Pan**, god of the woods, or **Hecate**, chthonic goddess, associated with childbirth, or the **Corybantes**, male attendants of Cybele, who was one manifestation of the **mountain mother**, imported from Anatolia.

146: **Dictynna**: a Cretan goddess identified with Artemis, at least in her role of "mistress of wild things."

148: **Mere**: most likely the precinct of Artemis Saronia (the Saronic Gulf was the body of water closest to Trozen) where the goddess had a shrine.

the noble-born leader of the Erechtheids,
with a union hidden from your marriage bed?
Or has a seafarer sailed   155
from Crete into the harbor
that is most welcoming to sailors,
with a message for the queen,
and she is bound to her bed
in grief over her troubles?   160

Epode

A bad, wretched helplessness
from labor pangs and mindlessness
is wont to dwell
with women's difficult temperament.
Once this breeze rushed through
my womb; I called to the heavenly   165
helper of labor, ruler of arrows,
Artemis, and, with the gods' blessing,
she always comes, making me envied.

The Nurse enters from the palace with Phaedra on a couch or bed carried by attendants.

Chorus Leader
Look, the old nurse brings her here,   170
outside the house before the doors.
A hateful cloud grows upon her brows.
My soul desires to learn what in the world it is—

153: **Erechtheids**: Athenians, descended from their legendary ruler Erechtheus.
154: **union hidden from your marriage bed**: Theseus had a deserved reputation as a philanderer.
157: **from Crete**: Phaedra was a native a Crete, the site of many unhappy passions. See below on 337.
168: **Artemis**: Patron of wild things, the hunt, and chastity, Artemis was also a goddess of childbirth.
170ff.: Phaedra arrives on stage from the palace on a couch carried by attendants, along with her Nurse. The object of the chorus' concern is now before their (and the audience's) eyes, but the revelation they seek proceeds on a circuitous course. This long scene (170-524) is broken up by changes in meter and structure (sustained speeches and rapid dialogue). The Nurse offers a conventional pragmatism, expressed with many platitudes, to contrast with Phaedra's high moral posture. Here she mixes complaints about her plight (caring for her mistress) with general reflections on the woes of humankind.

why the queen's complexion
has changed color.   175

Nurse

O the ills and hateful diseases of mortals!
What am I to do for you, what not to do?
Here is your daylight, here's your bright air.
Now the bed where you lie sick
is outside the house.   180
Your every word was to come here,
but soon you'll rush back into the house.
You're quickly frustrated and delight in nothing;
what's at hand doesn't please you, but whatever's absent
you think dearer.   185
It's better to be sick than to care for the sick:
the one is simple, but the other brings
both mental anguish and toil for the hands.
All life is painful for mortals
and there is no cease from toils.   190
  But whatever else is dearer than life,
darkness surrounds and hides it with clouds.
Indeed we clearly are madly in love
with this, whatever this is that shines on earth—
because of inexperience of another life   195
and the lack of revelation of the things beneath the earth;
we are carried along vainly by tales.

Phaedra

Lift up my body, hold my head upright!
My limbs are weak.
Seize my beautiful arms, attendants!   200
This head-dress on my head is heavy.
Take it off, spread out my locks on my shoulders!

198ff. Phaedra's excited lyrical expressions are confusing to the Nurse's lit-
    eral-mindedness. The contrast between the two is achieved in part
    through different rhythms. The Nurse speaks in "regular" anapests, as
    she has in the first part of this scene, while Phaedra's three central out-
    bursts (208-11, 215-22, and 228-32) are anapests, but of a more lyrical
    variety. Very likely they differed in delivery from the Nurse's lines.
202: **Take it off**: Removal of a woman's headdress symbolically suggested
    the loss of her chastity. Similarly, in letting down her hair, Phaedra might
    be seen as transgressive.

Nurse

  Take heart, child, and don't move
  your body so impatiently.
  You will bear the disease more readily   205
  with calm and a noble spirit.
  It is necessary for mortals to toil.

Phaedra

  Ah!
  How I wish I could draw a drink
  of pure water from a fresh spring,
  and lie down beneath poplars   210
  in a grassy meadow and take my rest!

Nurse

  Child, what are you crying aloud?
  Don't say these things before a crowd,
  hurling words mounted on madness.

Phaedra

  Take me to the mountains! I will go to the woods   215
  and to the pine trees, where the beast-slaying
  dogs run on the heels of dappled deer.
  Please, by the gods! I desire to shout to dogs,
  hold a pointed weapon in my hand
  and hurl a Thessalian spear   220
  past my yellow hair.

Nurse

  Why in the world, child, are you so distressed at heart?
  Why do *you* care about hunting?
  Why do you desire flowing spring water?   225
  There's a hillside with water here, near
  the city walls, where you could have a drink.

Phaedra

  Artemis, mistress of the sea's Mere
  and the hippodrome which resounds with hoof beats,
  I wish that I could be on your plain   230
  breaking in Enetic foals!

215ff. All the activities which Phaedra describes are associated with Hippolytus.

231: **Enetic**: The Enetoi, inhabitants of the area north of the Adriatic Sea,
    were famed for their horses.

Nurse

What now is this word you have hurled, out of your mind?
In your desire for the hunt, you set out just now
to go to the mountains, but now you desire
foals on the waveless sands.   235
These things need much divination
to tell what god is pulling on your reins
and knocking you out of your wits, child.

Phaedra

Wretched me, what in the world have I done?
Where have I wandered from good thinking?   240
I was mad, I fell because of ruin from a divinity.
Ah, ah, miserable one!
Dear Nurse, cover my head again;
I am ashamed of what I have said.
Cover me. Tears come from my eyes,   245
and my look is turned to shame.
To have one's thinking made straight is painful,
but madness is an evil. To die
without awareness is best.

Nurse

I'm covering you; but when will death   250
conceal *my* body?
A long life has taught me many things:
mortals should engage with one another
in moderate friendships
and not to the inmost marrow of the soul,   255
and the mind's affections should be able to be easily loosed—

241: **I was mad... ruin from a divinity**. Inexplicable behavior was commonly
   described as madness and ascribed to the gods. Passion was also frequently described as madness. The ruin (*ate*) that comes from the god
   does not excuse the human's responsibility for her/his actions.
243-4: **Cover my head...I am ashamed**: Aware that she has uttered a lyrical
   and cryptic expression of her desire for Hippolytus, Phaedra seeks to be
   covered up—a return to a "chaste" state. On shame in this play, see
   Essay, p. 69-71. Note also that Phaedra expresses her shame even at
   what she has said. This scene may well echo one from the earlier play, in
   which it seems that Hippolytus veiled his head in response to Phaedra's
   sexual overtures.
246: Probably a reference to blushing.

easy to push aside and to draw tight.
But for one person to labor over two,
as *I* feel pain for this one,
is a difficult burden.   260
They say that exacting conduct in life
brings about more falls than delight
and is at war more with health.
So I praise excessiveness less than
"nothing in excess;"   265
and the wise will agree with me.

Chorus Leader
Old woman, trusted nurse of the queen,
We see here Phaedra's wretched fortunes,
but it is unclear to us what her sickness is.
We would like to learn and hear about it from you.   270

Nurse
I don't know, despite my questions; she doesn't wish to tell.

Chorus Leader
Nor what the source of these pains is?

Nurse
You've come to the same point; she's silent about all these things.

Chorus Leader
How weak she is and how her body is wasted away!

Nurse
Of course, when it's been three days since she has eaten.   275

Chorus Leader
Because of some madness or trying to die?

Nurse
To die, you ask? This fasting *will* end her life.

Chorus Leader
What you say is remarkable, if her husband accepts this.

Nurse
She hides her pain and denies that she is sick.

265: **"nothing in excess":** This maxim, associated with Apollo's oracle at Delphi, was a commonplace of Greek life.
267: The scene now returns to the standard spoken meter of tragedy, iambic trimeter.

Chorus Leader

But can't he tell by looking at her face?   280

Nurse

No, he's actually abroad, away from this land.

Chorus Leader

But aren't *you* using force in trying
to learn about her sickness and the wandering of her wits?

Nurse

I've gone to all lengths and still have accomplished nothing.
Even so I will not now give up my zeal,   285
so that *you* may be present and bear witness to
how I am by nature to a mistress in misfortune.
      Come now, dear child, let's both forget
our earlier words. You become more pleasant
in loosening your gloomy brow and path of thought,   290
and where I didn't follow you well before,
I'll give that up and move on to better words.
And if you have a sickness that can't be spoken of,
women are here to help treat the disease.
But if your misfortune can be divulged to men,   295
speak, so that it can be mentioned to doctors.
      So, why are you silent? You shouldn't be silent, child,
but either refute me, if I say something wrong,
or agree with my good advice.
Say something. Look over here. Poor me!   300
Women, we labor at these toils in vain,
and we're no closer than before. For then she was not
softened by words and she is not persuaded now.
But know *this*—and then be more stubborn
than the sea—if you die, you will betray your   305
children, who won't have a share of their father's house.
No, by the Amazon, mistress of horses,
who gave birth to a master for your children,

281: Theseus is conveniently out of the country. In other versions of the story
    he is in Hades. In this play a simple visit to the oracle at Delphi accounts
    for his absence.
304-5: The sea's stubbornness was proverbial.
305-6: The Nurse wisely appeals to Phaedra through her children. Their abil-
    ity to succeed in life is prime motivation for Phaedra's actions; see 421-5.

a bastard who thinks he's legitimate, you know him well,
Hippolytus . . .

Phaedra

       Oh no!

Nurse

       Does this touch you?   310

Phaedra

You've destroyed me, dear nurse, and by the gods
I beg you to be silent from now on about this man.

Nurse

You see? You have your wits, but even though you do, you don't
wish to help your children and save your life.

Phaedra

I love my children; I am storm-tossed by another fortune.   315

Nurse

Are your hands pure of blood, child?

Phaedra

My hands are pure, but my mind is polluted.

Nurse

This isn't some harm conjured by an enemy, is it?

Phaedra

No, a dear one unwillingly destroys me unwilling.

Nurse

Theseus—has he wronged you?   320

Phaedra

May *I* not be seen doing him harm.

Nurse

So what is this terrible thing that incites you to die?

310: **Oh no**: Silent for more than sixty lines, Phaedra finally breaks her silence
at the mention of Hippolytus. Two changes of speakers in a single line of
iambic verse were extremely rare, thus underscoring the effect of this
moment of recognition and revelation.

317: This statement is remarkable in its attention to inward purity. Purity was
typically a matter of outward states, while mental purity was a concept
slow to develop in ancient Greece.

319: **unwillingly**: At this point Phaedra does not fault Hippolytus. This will
change after she hears his denunciation of women and attack on her
later in the play.

321: For this focus on appearances (**not be seen**) in ethical statements, see on 403-4.

Phaedra

Let me err; for I'm not erring against you.

Nurse

I will *not*, not willingly, but my failure will lie with you.

Phaedra

What are you doing? Are you using force, hanging
    upon my hand?   325

Nurse

Yes, and your knees, and I will never let go.

Phaedra

Bad, bad these things will be for you, wretched one,
    if you learn them.

Nurse

Why, what could be worse for me than not to succeed
    with you?

Phaedra

You will die. The deed, however, brings me honor.

Nurse

And then you hide it, although I'm supplicating
    for your good?   330

Phaedra

Yes; I'm trying to devise good from what's disgraceful.

Nurse

Won't you then appear more honorable if you speak?

Phaedra

Go away, please by the gods, and let go of my right hand!

Nurse

No, since you're not giving me the gift you ought.

Phaedra

I will give it, for I respect your supplication.   335

Nurse

I'll be silent now. From here the word is yours.

325: At this juncture, the Nurse takes Phaedra's hand and knees in a gesture
of ritual supplication. This act brought a socio-religious compulsion on
the supplicated to comply with the request. As is evident in this scene,
maintaining physical contact with the supplicated was essential. The
Nurse's desperation is seen in her taking this extreme act.

Phaedra
O wretched mother, what a passion you had!

Nurse
The one she had for the bull, child? Or what is this you're saying?

Phaedra
And you, my poor sister, wife of Dionysus!

Nurse
Child, what's wrong? Are you reviling your kin?   340

Phaedra
And I the third unfortunate one, how I'm dying!

Nurse
I'm alarmed. Where will this story end up?

Phaedra
From there, not recently, comes my misfortune.

Nurse
I'm no closer to knowing what I want to hear.

Phaedra
Ah! If only you could say for me what I must say!   345

Nurse
I am not a prophet who can know what's unclear surely.

Phaedra
What is this thing which they call people being in love?

Nurse
Something most pleasant, child, and painful at the same time.

Phaedra
My experience would be the second one.

Nurse
What are you saying? You're in love, child? With what man?   350

Phaedra
Whoever this one is, the Amazon's . . .

Nurse
You mean Hippolytus?

337: **Wretched mother:** Phaedra refers to her mother, Pasiphaë, who was struck with passion for a bull. At 339 she refers to her sister Ariadne, whose love affair with Dionysus ended (in some accounts) unhappily. Phaedra puts herself in the context of her family of unhappy Cretan women. In this play, unlike in the first version, Phaedra is determined *not* to fulfill her family's pattern of disastrous passion.

Phaedra

You hear this from yourself, not me.

Nurse

Oh no! What are you saying, child? How you've destroyed me!
Women, this is unendurable, I will not endure
living. I look upon a hateful day, a hateful light.   355
I will hurl my body, throw it down, I will die
and be free of life. Farewell, I am no more.
For those who are virtuous desire what's bad,
against their will but still they do. Cypris then is no god
but whatever else is greater than god,   360
who has destroyed Phaedra here, and me and the house.

Chorus Leader

Did you note—ah!—did you hear—ah!—
the wretched sufferings,
not to be heard, which the queen cried aloud?
May *I* die, dear one, before I arrive
at your state of mind! Oh no! Ah, ah!   365
Oh woman wretched because of these griefs!
Oh the pains that hold mortals!
You're ruined, you've brought to light what's evil.
What awaits you this whole day?
Something bad for the house will be accomplished.   370
It is no longer unclear where the fortune sent from Cypris
ends, o wretched child from Crete.

Phaedra

Women of Trozen, you who dwell
in this farthest forecourt of Pelops' land,

352: Phaedra never brings herself to say his name in this scene.

359-60: Here, and elsewhere in this play (see, e.g., 447ff. and 1268ff.), Aphrodite
is described as a force of nature as much as a god.

362-72: This brief lyric section (matched metrically at 669-79) divides this long
scene into smaller units.

373-430: In this long speech (her longest in the play), Phaedra explains the
course of her actions and the principles by which she has decided to take
her life. While many scholars have viewed this as Phaedra's articulation
of her moral failing, more recent interpretations see in this speech
Phaedra's expression of her high moral standards—and, implicitly, her
stark contrast with her counterpart in the earlier play.

374: **forecourt**: From her (normally) Athenian perspective, Phaedra imagines
Trozen as the "forecourt" of the Peloponnese, across the Saronic Gulf.

already at other times during night's long expanse   375
I have thought in general about the ruin of mortals' lives.
And they seem to me to do worse
not because of their natural judgment; for many are capable
of sensible thinking. No, we must look at it like this:
we know what's good and recognize it,   380
but we don't toil to accomplish it, some through laziness,
others because they prefer some pleasure
other than the good. There are many pleasures in life,
long conversations and leisure—a delightful evil—
and respect; and there are two kinds, one not bad,   385
the other a burden on the house. If what is appropriate were clear,
there would not be two with the same letters.
Since then this is in fact what I think,
there is no drug by which I was going to weaken
and fall into the opposite thinking.   390
    I will tell you my path of thought also.
When passion wounded me, I started to consider how
I might best bear it. So I began with this,
to keep quiet about this disease and conceal it;
for nothing can be trusted to the tongue, which knows how   395

379-81: Socrates, a contemporary of Euripides, asserted that no one willingly
    errs (the so-called Socratic paradox). Phaedra argues that in fact we often
    do know what is right, but fail to accomplish it for one reason or another.
    It is uncertain to what degree Euripides is responding directly to Socrates'
    argument, but at the very least the play is engaging with contemporary
    intellectual debates.
385: **respect**: *Aidos* may seem to sit oddly at the end of this list of pleasures,
    but from Phaedra's perspective it is what helps her to protect her good
    name.
385-6: **two kinds**: This phrase constitutes a major interpretative crux: are
    pleasure or respect of two kinds? The Greek does not allow for a defini-
    tive answer, but it is likely that the phrase refers to pleasures. At the
    same time, it is important to note that by its emphatic placement and
    thematic importance, respect stands out among these pleasures that can
    be both good and bad.
387: Either there would be one more word or one less thing. The statement
    reflects contemporary interest in the correctness of names.
388-90: These lines make clear that Phaedra's general thinking (see 376) ap-
    plies to her own situation.
395-7: This sentiment is shown to be painfully true in the following scene.

to admonish the thoughts of others,
but itself comes to possess the most evils by its own doing.
Secondly, I took care to bear the folly well,
trying to subdue it with moderation.
And third, when I couldn't manage   400
to master Cypris in these ways, it seemed to me good to die,
the best plan (no one will deny it).
For may I neither be unnoticed when I do good things,
nor have many witnesses when I do disgraceful ones.

I knew that the deed and the sickness brought a bad name,   405
and in addition to this I knew well that I was a woman,
an object of hatred to all. May she perish most wretchedly
whoever first began to disgrace her bed
with other men! It was from noble households
that this evil began among women.   410
For whenever what's disgraceful seems fine to the noble,
it will seem very much so to the base.
I also hate women who are chaste in reputation
but secretly have engaged in bad, reckless acts.
How in the world, Cypris, mistress from the sea,   415
can they look their spouses in the eye
and not shudder because the darkness, their accomplice,
and the timbers of the house might at some time speak.

This is the very thing that is killing me, dear ladies,
that I never be convicted of disgracing my husband   420
nor the children I gave birth to. No, may they flourish
and dwell in the famous city of Athens as free men
with free speech, with a good reputation in regard to their mother.
For this enslaves a man, even one who is boldhearted,

401-2: That dying was better than living poorly was a commonly expressed
  Greek sentiment.

403-4: Ancient Greece was what is frequently called a "shame culture," one in
  which excellence and its opposite were measured by external standards
  and one's worth was not easily distinguished from one's reputation. (See
  Essay, p. 69-71.) Phaedra is *not* suggesting here (or at 420-1) that she would
  tolerate her own improper behavior provided that she was not appre-
  hended. (Note her strong condemnation of hypocrisy at 413-4.) Rather
  she uses these phrases to express her repugnance at such behavior.

421-5: Phaedra is deeply concerned with her children's reputation as well. See
  717 and above on 305-6.

422: **free speech**: one of the most cherished of Athenian rights.

whenever he is aware of his mother's or father's wrong doings.   425
This alone, they say, contends with life—
having a just and good mind.
But time reveals the base among mortals, whenever it happens to,
placing a mirror before them, as before a young maiden;
may I never be seen in company with these.   430

Chorus Leader

Ah! Ah! Everywhere moderation is a fine thing
and harvests a good reputation among mortals!

Nurse

Lady, your situation just now scared me terribly for a moment.
But now I realize that I was foolish; and among mortals   435
second thoughts are somehow wiser.
For what you've experienced is nothing extraordinary
or unaccountable: the goddess's anger struck against you.
You're in love along with many mortals (what's remarkable
    about that?);
will you then destroy your life on account of passion?   440
Surely there is no advantage to those who desire others,
and those who are going to do so, if they must die.
For Cypris, when she flows greatly, is something that cannot be borne;
she goes gently after the one who yields,
but whomever she finds thinking extravagant and proud
    thoughts,   445
she takes him and you can't imagine how badly she treats him.
Cypris goes through the air
and is in the swell of the sea, everything is born from her;
she is the one who sows and gives desire,
from which all of us who live upon the earth are born.   450
    Now those who know the writings of the ancients
and themselves are constantly engaged in poetry

428-30: The speech's concluding image is provocative, evoking themes of
    both sexuality (the maiden's concern with her physical appearance) and
    revelation, which lie at the heart of this speech.
433-81: The Nurse has recovered and offers a rebuttal of Phaedra's view. She
    emphasizes what she views as common sense and yielding to the forces of
    nature. Conveniently for her argument, she focuses on passion in general
    and not the particulars of Phaedra's situation—union with her stepson.

know how Zeus once desired a union
with Semele, and they know how beautiful-shining Eos
once snatched Cephalus up into the company of the gods   455
because of desire; but still they dwell
in heaven and do not flee out of the way of the gods,
but they put up, I think, with being conquered by misfortune.
And *you* will not bear it? Your father then ought to have begotten you
on special conditions or under the rule of other gods,   460
if you will not put up with these laws.

How many indeed of those who are very sensible do you think,
when they see their marriage bed is sick, pretend not to?
And how many fathers help their errant
sons to bear their passion? For this is held as one of the
    wise principles   465
of mortals: what isn't good goes unnoticed.
Surely, mortals should not try too hard to perfect their lives;
and you wouldn't make too precise the roof
which covers a house. Since you've fallen into as much
misfortune as you have, how do you think you could swim out of it?   470
But if, being human, you have
more good than bad, you'd be very well off.

Come on, dear child, stop your poor thinking
and stop acting outrageously—for this is nothing other than
    outrage
wishing to be mightier than the gods—   475
and endure your passion; a god has willed this.
And even though you are sick, bring an end to your sickness
    in some good way.

453ff.: In support of her position, the Nurse uses two examples from well-
known myths to make an *a fortiori* argument: the gods suffer from
passion and endure, so too should mortals. In the first case, Zeus' union
with Semele led to the latter's incendiary destruction when Semele asked
her unidentified lover to appear to her in his full glory, the thunderbolt,
as it turned out. In the example of Eos' mortal lover Cephalus, the latter's
abandonment and decrepit aging (he received immortality but not eter-
nal youth) are fundamental to the tale. The Nurse omits any reference to
these unpleasant aspects of the stories.

464-5: The example of fathers helping their sons with their illicit romances
stands in ironic and tragic counterpoint to the events of the play.

471-2: This maxim, with its pessimistic view of human happiness, was commonly expressed in Greek literature.

There are incantations and bewitching words;
some drug for this sickness will appear.
Certainly men would be late in discovering contrivances,   480
if we women are not going to discover them.

Chorus Leader

Phaedra, she speaks more helpfully
for the present circumstances, but it's you I praise.
This praise, however, is harder to handle than
her words and more painful for you to hear.   485

Phaedra

This is what destroys well-governed cities
and the homes of mortals—overly fine words;
for one shouldn't speak what's pleasant to the ear
but what will give good repute.

Nurse

Why this lofty speech? It's not refined words   490
you need but the man. As quickly as possible we must
   understand things clearly,
speaking out about you frankly.
For if your life were not in such circumstances
and you were in fact a chaste woman,
I would never for the sake of your sexual pleasure   495
be leading you on to this point; but, as it is, the contest is a great one—
to save your life, and this shouldn't be begrudged.

Phaedra

You've spoken terrible things; won't you shut your mouth
and not utter such disgraceful words again?

478-9: The words are ambiguous—incantations and drugs either to drive
   away her passion or induce passion in the virgin Hippolytus.
486-524: In the concluding section of this long scene, the Nurse persuades
   Phaedra to let her act on her mistress' behalf. The contrast presented in
   the two positions defined in their two speeches is now seen in the thrust
   and parry of dialogue. The Nurse persuades Phaedra through highly
   ambiguous speech. Throughout this exchange there is a deliberate lack
   of clarity as to what the Nurse is planning to do. Phaedra expressly
   forbids the Nurse to talk to Hippolytus (520) but is weary and weakened
   enough (note 504-6) to allow the Nurse to act in some way on her behalf.
   The playwright is thus able to suggest that Phaedra is no party to the
   Nurse's scheming while creating suspense as to what will happen next.
486-7: This condemnation of rhetoric is found frequently in contemporary literature, a response to the increasingly important role it played in Athenian life.

Nurse

> Disgraceful, but these are better for you than fine ones;   500
> and the deed is better, if it will save you,
> than the name, in which you will exult and die.

Phaedra

> Ah! Don't, by the gods—for you speak well but disgracefully—
> go beyond this, since my soul is well tilled
> by passion, and if you speak finely about what's disgraceful   505
> I will be consumed by what I'm now fleeing.

Nurse

> Fine, if this seems best to you . . . you ought not to be erring,
> but if in fact you are, obey me; the favor is second best.
> I have in the house love-charms that are enchantments
> for passion, and it just occurred to me   510
> that they will stop you from this disease
> without disgrace and without harming your mind, if you don't
>   become cowardly.
> But we need to get some token of that one who's desired,
> either a lock of hair or something from his garments,
> and join together one delight from two.   515

Phaedra

> Is this remedy something applied or drunk?

Nurse

> I don't know. Wish to profit, child, not to learn.

Phaedra

> I'm afraid that you'll appear too clever for me.

Nurse

> Know that you'd fear everything. What *do* you fear?

Phaedra

> Please don't mention any of this to Theseus' offspring.   520

Nurse

> Let it be, child. I'll arrange these things well.
> Only may you, mistress from the sea, Cypris,

522-4: Most likely Phaedra (the character, not the actor playing her) did not hear the Nurse's closing words. One of the conventions of the fifth-century stage allowed one character to break off contact with another without the second character hearing the first's following words. Here the Nurse has stopped speaking to Phaedra and addresses Aphrodite's statue.

be my accomplice. The other things I have in mind
it will suffice to tell friends within.

The Nurse exits into the palace.

Chorus:

Strophe A

Eros, Eros, you who drip desire   525
down into the eyes as you lead sweet delight
into the souls of those you war against,
never may you appear to me with harm
or come out of measure.
For the shaft neither of fire nor of the stars is superior   530
to Aphrodite's, which Eros, the son of Zeus,
sends forth from his hands.

Antistrophe A

In vain, in vain along the Alpheus   535
and in the Pythian home of Phoebus
the <land> of Hellas slaughters more and more oxen,
but Eros, the tyrant of men,
the holder of the keys to Aphrodite's
dearest inner chambers, we do not venerate,   540

525-64: The first *stasimon*. As the Nurse is inside propositioning (as it turns out)
Hippolytus and before we learn of these actions, the chorus sing of Eros'
power, while Phaedra is by the palace door. This song has a common
structure: two stanzas on a general theme (the destructive power of Eros)
followed by two with specific examples of this principle (Zeus and Semele
and Heracles and Iole). The Trozenian women focus on the destructive
power of passion, or, more particularly, illicit passion. See Essay, p. 73-4.

525-34: The opening of this song echoes the form of cult hymns; for the
language, see above on 61-71. **Eros**: The son of Aphrodite and (depending on the myth) various fathers, Eros is here depicted as a warrior. His
arrow was a common attribute; the military images are more fully developed here. Frequently, there is little functional difference between
Eros and Aphrodite, as here the first half of the song sings about the
power of Eros, while the second half refers to Aphrodite.

526: **down into the eyes**: the eyes were imagined as both the site of erotic
desire and the source of infatuation.

535: **Alpheus**: major river that flowed through Olympia, the site of the Olym-
pic games and one of Zeus' main shrines.

536: **Phoebus**: the god Apollo, who had a prominent shrine in Delphi (in
central Greece), which could be referred to with the adjective Pythian.

although he destroys mortals and sends them through every misfortune whenever he comes.

Strophe B

The filly in Oechalia,   545
unyoked in marriage,
with no man and no wedding before, Cypris
yoked her away from Eurytus' house,
like a running Naiad or a Bacchant,
with blood, with smoke,   550
in a bloody wedding,
and gave her away in marriage to Alcmene's son. Oh
wretched in your wedding!

Antistrophe B

Holy wall   555
of Thebes and mouth of Dirce,
you could confirm how Cypris is when she comes.
Giving the mother of twice-born Bacchus
in marriage
to a flaming thunderbolt,   560
she brought her to sleep in a bloody doom.
For she is terrible, and blows on all there is, and like
a bee she flits.

Phaedra is standing near the palace door.

Phaedra
Silence, women! We are destroyed.   565

Chorus Leader
What in the house terrifies you, Phaedra?

Phaedra
Hold on. Let me learn fully what those within are saying.

545-54: Heracles was infatuated with Iole, daughter of Eurytus, king of
    Oechalia. When Eurytus refused to give his daughter in marriage to
    Heracles after he had won an archery contest with her as prize, Heracles
    destroyed his city.
555-64: For the story of Semele, native of Thebes, and Zeus, see above on 453ff.
556: **Dirce**: a famous Theban spring.
565-600: In this exchange, Phaedra speaks almost exclusively in "calm" iambic
    rhythms, while the chorus express their anxiety and excitement in lyrics.

Chorus Leader
I'm silent. But this is an inauspicious prelude.

Phaedra
Woe is me!
Ah! Wretched because of my sufferings.   570

Chorus Leader
What speech are you crying aloud, what words are you shouting?
Tell me what report rushes over your mind
and scares you, lady.

Phaedra
We're ruined. Stand by these gates   575
and hear the clamor that falls within the house.

Chorus Leader
You're by the door, it's your job to convey
the talk within the house.
Tell me, tell me, *what* is the trouble that has come?   580

Phaedra
The child of the horse-loving Amazon, Hippolytus,
cries aloud, reviling my attendant terribly.

Chorus Leader
I hear a voice, but I have nothing clear.   585
Shout out what sort of cry has come,
come through the gates to you.

Phaedra
Look, now he clearly declares her "matchmaker of evils,"
"betrayer of your master's bed."   590

Chorus Leader
Woe is me for these ills!
You are betrayed, my dear.
What can I devise for you?
For what was hidden has been revealed. You're ruined—
ah!, woe, woe!—betrayed by friends.   595

Phaedra
By speaking of my misfortunes she destroyed me,
trying to cure this disease, as a friend but improperly.

Chorus Leader
What now? What will you do, you who have suffered what
can't be remedied?

Phaedra

I don't know, except one thing—to die as quickly as possible;
this is the only cure for my present miseries. 600

Phaedra withdraws from the palace door, but does not exit.

Hippolytus enters from the palace, followed by the Nurse.

Hippolytus

O mother earth, and the sun-filled sky,
what unspeakable words I heard uttered!

Nurse

Be quiet, child, before someone hears your cry!

Hippolytus

It's not possible to be silent, when I've heard terrible things.

Nurse

Yes, I beg you by this fair right arm of yours. 605

Hippolytus

Don't bring your hand near me, don't touch my robes!

Nurse

Oh, I beg you by your knees, *don't* destroy me!

Hippolytus

Why do you say that if, as you say, you've spoken nothing bad?

Nurse

That conversation, child, was *not* for all.

Hippolytus

Surely what's good is better when spoken among many. 610

Nurse

Child, *don't* dishonor your oath!

599-600: It should be noted that at this point Phaedra's plan is still to die (as quickly as possible); vengeance on Hippolytus becomes an issue only after the following scene.

600: *Phaedra . . . does not exit*. The staging of this scene is controversial. Some critics, in order to account for Phaedra's apparent misunderstanding of Hippolytus' intentions, assume that she departs and then returns at the end of the scene. But this would be very much opposed to what we know of fifth-century practice. Most likely, Phaedra remains on stage and effectively serves as the silent, indirect and obvious object of Hippolytus' attack. In the only scene in which these two characters appear on stage together, they do not acknowledge each other's presence.

605: The Nurse attempts (unsuccessfully) to supplicate Hippolytus, as she had (successfully) supplicated Phaedra; see above on 325.

Hippolytus
My tongue is sworn, my mind unsworn.

Nurse
Child, what will you do? Will you destroy your friends?

Hippolytus
I spit this out! No one who's unjust is a friend of mine.

Nurse
Forgive; it is natural for humans to err, child.   615

Hippolytus
Zeus, why did you establish women in the sun's light
as counterfeit, an evil for human beings?
If you wanted to propagate the human race,
you should not have provided this from women,
but mortals ought to place bronze or iron   620
or a weight of gold in your temples
and buy offspring in exchange for a set value,
each one for its price,
and then dwell in their homes free, with no females.
[But, as it is, first of all, when we are about to lead an evil   625
into the house, we pay out the wealth of the house.]
And this is how it's clear that a woman is a great evil:
a father who has begotten and reared her, gives a dowry in
     addition,
and sends her out of the house so he can be rid of the evil.
And the man who in turn takes this ruinous creature into his
     house   630
rejoices when he adds a pretty ornament
to the worst statue, and he toils, wretched one,
to deck her out with robes, while draining the prosperity of the
     house.
[This has to happen: he marries well

612: A line parodied several times by the comic playwright and Euripidean
     contemporary Aristophanes. It is also not Hippolytus' considered opin-
     ion, as he makes clear later in this scene (656ff.), but it expresses his
     disgust and outrage at the Nurse's proposal.
618-24: This bizarre wish reflects both contemporary misogyny and is paral-
     leled elsewhere in Euripides. For all its extremity, this wish is in keeping
     with Hippolytus' extraordinary rejection of sex and marriage, and, it
     should be remembered, is the young man's initial response to what he
     believes to be his stepmother's sexual overture.

and enjoying his in-laws keeps for himself a bitter marriage
    bed,   635
or getting a good marriage and harmful in-laws
he suppresses the misfortune with the good.]
It's easiest for the man who has a "nothing;" but a woman
set up foolishly in the house is harmful.
And I hate a clever woman; not in my house   640
may there be one with more thoughts than a woman should have.
For Cypris engenders wickedness more often
in the clever ones; the clueless woman
is deprived of foolish wantonness by her slight intelligence.
A servant should not go indoors to a woman,   645
but one should set up voiceless savage beasts to dwell with them,
so that they can neither address anyone
nor in turn hear any word from them.
But, as things are, they devise evil plans   650
within, and servants carry them outside.
    So you too, evil one, you came
to traffic with me about my father's undefiled marriage bed.
I will wash these things away with flowing river water,
splashing it against my ears. *How* could I be base,
who feel impure just hearing such things?   655
But know well, woman, my piety saves you:
if I hadn't been caught off guard by taking oaths to the gods,
I would never have kept from declaring this to my father.
But, as things are, I will go away from the house so long
    as Theseus
is out of the country, and I will keep my mouth silent.   660
But I'll return when my father does
and I will watch how you look at him, you and that mistress
    of yours.
[I will know that I have tasted your daring.]
May you both perish! I will never have my fill of hating
women, not even if someone says that I'm always saying this. 665
For truly they too are always somehow evil.
Either then let someone teach them to be chaste,
or let *me* always trample on them.

645ff.: A thinly veiled attack on the Nurse's action.

659-62: The dynamics of the plot require Hippolytus' absence from the next part
    of the drama, just as they were helped by Theseus' absence in the first half.

Hippolytus exits down the eisodos *by which he first entered*

Phaedra

    Oh wretched, ill-fated

    destinies of women! What device or word do we have,   670

    now that we've been tripped up, to loose the knot of words?

    We've met with retribution. Oh earth and light!

    Wherever will I escape this fortune?

    How, friends, will I hide my pain?

    What god could appear as a helper, what mortal   675

    as an ally or accomplice in unjust deeds?

    For my trouble

    goes across the boundary of life—a difficult crossing.

    I am the most ill-fated of women.

Chorus Leader

    Ah, ah, it's all over, and your servant's schemes,   680

    lady, have failed; things go badly.

Phaedra

    O most evil one and destroyer of friends,

    what you've done to me! May my ancestor Zeus

    strike you with fire and destroy you by the roots.

    Didn't I tell you—didn't I anticipate your mind?—   685

    to be silent about the things about which I'm now disgraced?

    But you didn't control yourself; so no longer will I die

    with a good reputation. Ah, I need new words:

    for this man, his mind whetted by anger,

    will denounce me to his father for your errors,   690

    will tell aged Pittheus the situation,

    and will fill the entire land with the most disgraceful words.

    May you perish, you and whoever is eager

    to give improper help to unwilling friends!

669-79: Phaedra's brief lament matches metrically the chorus leader's lyrics at 362ff. At 680, the characters return to regular spoken iambics.

672: **we've met with retribution**: The phrase need not mean that Phaedra imagines she is being justly punished, only that she recognizes that she has met with retaliation.

683: **ancestor Zeus**: Phaedra's father, Minos, was son of Zeus and Europa.

688: **new words**: The first hint of her planned response to Hippolytus' denunciation.

Nurse

Mistress, you can fault what I did wrong, 695
for this biting pain conquers your judgment.
But I too can speak to this, if you'll accept it.
I reared you and am devoted to you; while seeking remedies
for your disease I found not what I wished.
But if I had fared well, indeed I'd be held among the wise. 700
For we get a reputation for intelligence in proportion to our fortune.

Phaedra

What?! Is this just and satisfactory for me,
that you wound me and then give way in words?

Nurse

We're talking too much. I wasn't moderate.
But it's possible, child, to be saved even from this. 705

Phaedra

Stop talking. You didn't give me good advice
before and what you attempted was evil.
But go, out of the way, and take thought
for yourself; I will arrange my own things well.

The Nurse exits into the palace.

But you, noble-born children of Trozen, 710
grant me this request at least:
conceal in silence what you have heard here.

Chorus Leader

I swear by proud Artemis, daughter of Zeus,
that I will never reveal any of your ills to light.

Phaedra

Well spoken—thank you. I will tell you one thing further: 715
I have a remedy for this misfortune
so that I can hand over a life of fair repute to my children
and myself profit considering how things have fallen out.
For I will never disgrace my Cretan home,
nor will I come before Theseus' face 720
with disgraceful deeds done, for the sake of one life.

709: A strong echo of the Nurse's words at 521 with the addition of **my own**.
712: Because of their constant presence, the chorus' complicity is necessary for plotting on stage.
717-21: Phaedra states her prime motivation—ensuring her children's good name and avoiding disgrace.

Chorus Leader
What incurable ill are you about to *do*?

Phaedra
To die; but how—this I will plan.

Chorus Leader
Speak no words of bad omen.

Phaedra
                    And you, give me no bad advice.
In being rid of my life this day, I will delight   725
Cypris, the very one who destroys me.
I will be worsted by a bitter passion.
But in death I will be a bane for the other,
so that he may learn not to be haughty
at my ills; and by sharing this disease   730
in common with me he will learn to be moderate.

Phaedra exits into the palace.

Chorus:

Strophe A
May I be within the hidden recesses of the steep mountain;
there may a god make me
a winged bird among the flying flocks!
And may I fly high
over the sea waves of the Adrian coast   735
and the water of the Eridanus,
where the unhappy girls drip amber-gleaming tears

728-31: Immediately before she exits to kill herself, Phaedra enunciates a
     further motivating force—vengeance against Hippolytus for his haugh-
     tiness over her. The Greeks upheld a code of "help friends/harm en-
     emies," one facet of which was that an enemy's gloating over one's
     misfortunes was intolerable. Just as Hippolytus has implicitly rejected
     Phaedra as a "friend" (see 613-4), so too will Phaedra treat him as an
     enemy, and by this code will seek vengeance against him.
731: An echo of Hippolytus' words at 666.
732-75. Often called an "escape ode," the second *stasimon* expresses the cho-
     rus' anxiety in response to Phaedra's ominous departure. Structurally its
     four stanzas fall into two halves, the first fanciful and mythological, the
     second historical and, then, immediate.
735: **Adrian coast**: Gulf of Venice
737: **Eridanus**: fabulous river in the far west, later identified with the Po.

into the dark-colored swell   740
in lamentation over Phaethon!

Antistrophe A

May I reach the apple-sown shore
of the Hesperides, the singers,
where the lord of the sea's dark-colored mere
no longer provides a path for sailors,   745
but ordains a holy boundary
of heaven, which Atlas holds,
and the ambrosial springs flow past where Zeus lay,
where very holy earth, the giver of prosperity,   750
increases blessedness for the gods!

Strophe B

O white-winged Cretan
ship, you who conveyed my mistress
from her prosperous home
through the roaring sea waves of the deep,   755
a delight that proved most ruinous for the marriage.
For indeed there were evil omens at both ends of her journey—
both when she flew from the land of Crete to glorious Athens
and when they tied the woven rope-ends to the
    shores of Munichus   760
and stepped onto the mainland.

Antistrophe B

Because of this her wits were crushed
by a terrible disease   765
of impious passion from Aphrodite.

738-41: **Phaethon**: The son of Helius, the sun god, he doubted his paternity
and asked to steer the god's chariot as proof. This trip ended in catastrophe and Phaethon's sisters were turned into poplar trees, shedding am-
ber as their tears.

742: **Hesperides**: These were commonly depicted as singers and served as
the guardians of the garden where the golden apples given to Hera as a
wedding gift from her grandmother Ge (Earth) were planted. **where
Zeus lay** (749) seems to refer to his original lovemaking with Hera.

747: **Atlas** traditionally held up the earth and was connected with the golden
apples in various stories.

757: The Greeks were very sensitive to omens, especially connected to an
important event, such as the departure and arrival of Theseus' ship.

760: **Munichus**: the eponymous hero of the older port of Attica, the Munichia.

And foundering under this hard misfortune she will attach
a suspended noose from the bridal chamber's beams,
fitting it around her white neck,   770
since she feels shame at her hateful fortune,
and chooses instead a repute of good fame and rids
her mind of its painful passion.   775

Nurse Within

Oh! Oh!
Everybody around the palace, come and help!
Our mistress, the wife of Theseus, is hanging.

Chorus Leader

Ah, ah! It's all over. The queen is no more,
hanging in a suspended noose.

Nurse Within

Won't you hurry? Won't someone bring a two-edged   780
blade so we can loose this knot around her neck?

Chorus Leader

Friends, what should we do? Do you think we should enter the
    house
and free the queen from the tightly drawn noose?

Another Chorus Member

What?! Aren't young servants at hand?
Meddling doesn't bring safety in life.   785

Nurse Within

Stretch out the wretched corpse and make it straight;
this was a bitter tending of the home for my master.

Chorus Leader

The unhappy woman is dead, from what I hear:
they're already stretching her out as a corpse.

Theseus enters from one of the eisodoi.

767ff.: Most unusually, the chorus express an almost clairvoyant picture of
    what the audience will soon witness. In general, in Greek myth and
    literature, women kill themselves by hanging and not by the sword.

771-5: These lines provide a concise and powerful summary of Phaedra's
    major concerns presented in the first half of the play.

776-89: A voice from within (presumably the Nurse's) is heard, proclaiming
    Phaedra's death, while the chorus hesitate to take action. The fact of the
    queen's death is thus established (immediately) before Theseus' return
    to the palace.

Theseus

Women, do you know what in the world is the servants' shouting
~ ringing deeply~ in the house that has reached me?   790
For the house doesn't see fit to open its doors
and give me a friendly greeting upon my return from the oracle.
It can't be that something bad has happened to old Pittheus, can it?
His life is already advanced, but even so   795
his departure from this house would be painful to me.

Chorus Leader

Your misfortune doesn't concern the old,
Theseus; the death of the young pains you.

Theseus

Oh no! It's not my children's life that is plundered, is it?

Chorus Leader

They're alive, but their mother is dead, the most painful
       thing possible for you.   800

Theseus

What are you saying? My wife is dead? By what fortune?

Chorus Leader

She fixed a suspended noose to hang herself.

Theseus

Chilled by grief or from what misfortune?

Chorus Leader

We know only so much; for I too just arrived at the house,
Theseus, to mourn your troubles.   805

Theseus

Ah! Why am I wreathed with these plaited leaves
on my head, since my visit to the oracle brought me misfortune?
Open the doors of the gate, servants,
unloose their fastenings, so I may see the bitter sight
of my wife, who in dying has destroyed me.   810

804-5: Their vow of complicit silence requires this lie to Theseus.

806-7: Theseus wears a garland of leaves in connection with his visit to the oracle. His tearing it up contrasts with Hippolytus offering a garland to Artemis in the play's opening.

810: In response to Theseus' command, the doors are opened and Phaedra's body revealed. This is accomplished by means of the *ekkyklema*, a wheeled platform that allowed for interior scenes to be made visible to the audience and on-stage characters. Once on stage, Phaedra's corpse serves as the physical object

As the chorus sing, the ekkyklema *is wheeled out with Phaedra's corpse.*

Chorus
Oh, oh wretched one because of your miserable ills!
You suffered, you did
so much that you've confounded the house.
Ah for your reckless daring—
you died violently and by an unholy misfortune
in a wrestling match with your own miserable hand!   815
Who, wretched one, consigns your life to darkness?

Theseus
Woe for my pains! I, wretched me, have suffered
the greatest of my ills. O fortune,
how heavily you've come upon me and the house,
an unperceived stain from some malignant spirit—
no, you're the destruction that makes my life unlivable!   820
O wretch, I see a sea of ills so great
that I will never swim back out of it
or pass through the wave of this misfortune.
With what word, wife, with which one shall I, wretched me,
correctly address your heavy-fated fortune?
For like a bird you are vanished from my hands,
you rushed from me with a swift leap to Hades.
Ah, ah, miserable, miserable are these sufferings!   830
From somewhere long ago I am recovering
a fortune sent by the divinities because of the faults
of some ancestor.

Chorus Leader
Not to you alone have these ills come, lord,

---

of Theseus' grief and, with the soon-to-be-discovered note, the damning proof (in his father's eyes) of Hippolytus' guilt. It also serves as a potent visual backdrop to the debate between father and son later in this scene.

811-55. Theseus' lamentation and the choral comments are all in lyric meters.

819: Like many characters in Greek tragedy, Theseus suggests that his misfortune comes from an avenging spirit, stirred most likely (see also 831ff. and 1379ff.) by an ancestral crime. "The sins of the fathers are visited on the sons." Whereas in some dramas, the motif of an avenging spirit is fully developed, in this play it appears more as a commonplace to express the incomprehensible and is not woven into the play's fabric.

834-5: Statements such as these were the stock phrases of consolation, no more effective in Euripides' time than in our own.

but along with many others you have lost your cherished wife. 835

Theseus

Beneath the earth, beneath the earth, I want to die,
move to the gloom there and dwell in darkness, oh wretched me,
since I am bereft of your dearest companionship.
For you destroyed more than you perished.
From where, wretched wife,   840
did this deadly fortune come to your heart?
Could someone say what happened, or is it in vain that
the royal house holds a throng of my servants?
Woe is me, <wretched> because of you,
<woe,> what a pain I have seen for the house,   845
unendurable, unspeakable! Oh, I'm destroyed.
The house is empty, and the children are orphaned.
<Ah, ah!> You left, you left us, o dear
and best of women, of however many
the light of the sun and night's starry-faced   850
brightness look upon.

Chorus

O wretched Theseus, how much ill this house holds;
my eyes are wet with floods of tears at your fortune.
But I've been shuddering for some time at the calamity
to come.   855

Theseus

Ah, ah!
What is this tablet hanging
from her dear hand? Does it wish to declare something new?
What—did the unhappy one write me a letter about our
marriage bed
and children, asking for something?

856ff.: The meter returns to spoken (iambic) rhythm as Theseus discovers the
tablet attached to Phaedra's wrist. When he discovers what the tablet
reveals, he breaks out again in lyric rhythms (874ff.) until the point at
which he formally declares Hippolytus' crime and punishment. The chorus leader also delivers his words in lyric meters, returning to spoken
meter after Theseus does.

856: **tablet**: The note left on the tablet is a convenient plot device, allowing
Phaedra to communicate (falsely) with her husband. Intensity is added to
the scene by the personification of the tablet (see 857, 863 and 877-80) and
the irony of what Theseus imagines it will reveal and what it in fact does.

Take heart, wretched one: there is no woman   860
who will come into Theseus' bed and house.
Look, the impression of the dead woman's
gold-wrought seal here seeks my attention.
Come, let me unwind the strings of the seal
and see what this tablet wishes to say to me.   865

Chorus Leader

Ah, ah, a god brings in this further,
new ill in succession. ~In light of what has happened,
what terrible thing could there be to meet with?~
For ruined, no longer living, I say—
ah, ah!—is my masters' house.   870
[O spirit, if it's somehow possible, don't overturn the house,
but listen to my prayer;
for from somewhere I see, like a prophet, a bird of bad omen.]

Theseus

Oh woe! What an ill upon ill this is, another one,
unendurable, unspeakable! Oh wretched me!   875

Chorus Leader

What is it? Tell me, if I may be told at all.

Theseus

The tablet cries out, cries out insufferable things. Where can I
    escape
the weight of ills? For I'm gone, ruined,
since I've seen, wretched me, such, such a song
taking voice in writing.   880

Chorus Leader

Ah! You are revealing a word that is the leader of ills.

Theseus

I will no longer keep this destructive,
hard-to-express evil within the gates of my mouth.
O city!
Hippolytus dared to touch my marriage bed   885
by force, showing no honor for the revered eye of Zeus.

862-5: Phaedra's tablet was two pieces of wood, coated with wax for inscription and connected by a hinge. It was wound with string and sealed with wax and the "signature" of an embossed ring.

886: Zeus was concerned with upholding justice in general and, among many other things, marriage in particular (despite his own infidelities).

Father Poseidon, you once promised me
three curses; with one of these
make an end of my son, and may he not escape this
day, if the curses you gave me are sure.   890

Chorus Leader
Lord, by the gods, take this back and undo this prayer;
for you will recognize later that you erred. Listen to me.

Theseus
Impossible. And in addition I will drive him from this land,
and he will be stricken by one of two fates:
either Poseidon will revere my curses   895
and send him dead into the house of Hades,
or exiled from this country he will wander
over a foreign land and drag out a painful life.

Chorus Leader
Look, here your son Hippolytus himself is at hand,
at just the right moment. Relax your evil anger, lord   900
Theseus, and plan what's best for your house.

*Hippolytus enters with some attendants by the same eisodos by
which he departed.*

Hippolytus
I heard your shout, father, and came
quickly. And I still don't know what
you're groaning over; but I'd like to hear it from you.
Ah! What's this? Your wife, father, I see that she is   905
dead. This is most remarkable:
I just left her; she saw this light not long ago.
What has happened to her? How did she perish?

887-90: Three curses (or wishes) are a folktale motif, adopted by this myth. Not having used one of them before, Theseus is uncertain of their efficacy. So, he immediately follows this curse with his own proclamation of exile.

902ff. With Hippolytus' arrival, the scene is set for a debate between him and his father. Almost all of Euripides' plays contained such a formalized debate (commonly called an *agon*), reflecting the increasing contemporary interest in rhetoric and the practice of the law courts. The "prosecutor" (Theseus) goes first, the "defendant" (Hippolytus) second, their long speeches punctuated by a bland choral comment and followed by rapid dialogue between them.

Father, I wish to learn from you.   910
You're silent. But there is no place for silence in troubles.
[For the heart desiring to hear everything
even in troubles is convicted of being greedy.]
It is not just, father, for you to conceal your misfortunes
from your *friends* and those even more than friends.   915

Theseus

O mankind, so often wrong and useless,
why do you teach countless skills
and devise and discover everything,
but one thing you do not know nor have you yet tracked down—
to teach good sense to those who have none?   920

Hippolytus:

You're talking about a clever man who can compel
those who don't have good sense to have it.
But you're being subtle at an inappropriate moment, father,
and I fear that your speech goes too far because of your troubles.

Theseus

Ah, mortals ought to have established a sure sign   925
of friends and a means of distinguishing their minds,
to tell who is a true friend and who isn't.
And all men ought to have two voices,
one just, the other how it happened to be,
so that the one thinking unjust things could be refuted   930
by the just one; and we would not be deceived.

Hippolytus

What?! Has some friend slandered me to you,
and am I afflicted with this sickness, when I am not at all
    responsible?
I'm alarmed: your words go astray,
beyond sense, and alarm me.   935

Theseus

Ah, mortal mind!—where will it end up?
What limit will there be to its daring and over-boldness?
For if generation after generation
it will expand, and the next one will surpass in wickedness

920: On learned versus innate qualities, see above on 79-80.
928ff. Another fanciful wish (see 618ff.), inspired perhaps by ventriloquism.

the one that went before, the gods will have to attach   940
another land to earth to contain
those who are by nature unjust and evil.
Look at this man, who, though born from me,
disgraced my marriage bed and is convicted
clearly by this dead woman of being most evil.   945
    But, since I've already come into pollution, show
your face here, before your father.
You consort with the gods as a superior man?
You are virtuous and pure of evils?
I couldn't be persuaded by your boasts   950
so that I think poorly and attribute ignorance to the gods.
Now pride yourself and through your vegetarian diet
be a huckster with your food, and with Orpheus as lord
play the bacchant and honor many vaporous writings—
for you're caught. I proclaim to everyone   955
to flee from such men as these; for they hunt you down
with their solemn words, while they devise disgraceful deeds.
    This woman is dead; do you think that this will save you?
In this most of all you're convicted, o you most evil one:
for what sort of oaths, what arguments could be stronger   960
than this woman here, so that you escape the charge?
Will you say that she hated you, and, of course, that the bastard
is naturally at war with the legitimate offspring?
You're saying that she's a bad merchant of her life,
if she destroyed what's dearest because of her enmity
    towards you.   965
Or will you say that sexual folly is not inherent in men,
but in women? I know that young men
are no less likely to fall than women,
whenever Cypris stirs up a young mind;
and the fact that they're male helps them.   970

951ff: It is clear from the opening scene (109-11) that Hippolytus is no veg-
    etarian. This and the facile references to Orpheus (legendary character
    around whom a cult arose) and Dionysiac religion ("play the bacchant,"
    a bacchant being a female devotee of the god of wine and the sap of life,
    Dionysus) suggest that Theseus is relying merely on the caricature of a
    "holy man" to attack his son.
962-3: On the theme of illegitimacy in this play, see above on 10, and Intro-
    duction, p. xxii.

Now then—why do I contend like this with your arguments
when the corpse before us is the surest witness?
Get out of this land as an exile as quickly as possible,
and don't go to god-built Athens
nor the boundaries of the land my spear holds sway over.   975
For if after suffering these things I am to be worsted by you,
Isthmian Sinis will never bear witness
that I killed him but say that I boast in vain,
and the Scironian rocks that border on the sea
will deny that I am harsh to the wicked.   980

Chorus Leader
I don't know how I could say that any mortal is
fortunate; for what was highest is turned upside down.

Hippolytus
Father, the fierceness and intensity of your mind are
terrible; but if someone should unfold this matter,
though it has fine words, it is not fine.   985
I am unaccomplished at giving speeches before a crowd,
but more skilled before a few of my peers;
and this too is natural: for those who are inadequate
in the presence of the wise are more eloquent at speaking
        before a crowd.
But nevertheless, since this disaster has come, I must   990
speak. And I will first begin my speech
where you first tried to catch me,

977: **Isthmian Sinis**. Sinis, an inhabitant of the Corinthian Isthmus, was one
    of many thugs dispatched by Theseus on his original journey from Trozen
    to Athens.
979: **Scironian rocks**: The brigand Sciron gave his name to these cliffs (on the
    Saronic coast of the Isthmus) after being killed by Theseus by being
    hurled from them.
983-1035: Hippolytus, with no physical evidence and unwilling to break his
    oath, has little with which to mount his defense. So he relies on asser-
    tions of his virtue and arguments from probability—how it was unlikely
    that he could have done this deed. Such arguments do not disprove the
    "facts" of the case, of course, but were popular in contemporary ora-
    tory.
986-7: A commonplace of Greek rhetoric, but also a reflection of Hippolytus'
    narrow range of experience. Fifth-century Athens was very much a
    public community in which citizens were expected to play an active part
    in the life of the city.

seeking to demolish me without a chance to reply. You see this light
and earth; in these there is no man—
even if you should deny it—more virtuous by nature than me. 995
For I know first of all how to revere the gods
and to associate with friends who do not attempt wrong
but who would be ashamed either to give evil commands
    to their friends or
to repay disgraceful deeds in kind;
I am not someone who laughs at his companions, father, 1000
but the same to friends when they're away as when nearby.
And by one thing I am untouched, the thing by which you
    now think you have me:
to this very moment my body is pure of sex.
I don't know this deed except by hearing of it in stories
and seeing it in pictures; for I am not eager 1005
even to look at these things, since I have a virgin soul.
    Suppose my chastity does not persuade you; let it go.
You *must* show in what way I was corrupted.
Was it that her body was more beautiful
than that of all women? Or did I expect, if I took 1010
an heiress as wife, that I would dwell as lord in your house?
I was a fool then, no, completely out of my mind.
Or will you say that rule is sweet? For those who are sensible
~not at all, unless~ it has destroyed the mind
of those mortals who like monarchy. 1015
But I would like to be first at victories
in the Hellenic games, but in the city second,
prospering always with the best as friends.
For this has political power, and the absence of danger
gives a delight greater than rule. 1020
    One of my arguments hasn't been spoken, you have the rest:
if I had a witness to my true character
and I were being tried while this woman saw the light,
you would have seen who was base by examining them
    with the facts.
But, as things stand, by Zeus of oaths and by the plain of earth, 1025

1010-1: Legally (from the perspective of fifth-century law), Hippolytus would have
    no claim on Theseus' rule by virtue of marriage to Phaedra. But in myth (see
    the stories of Jocasta, Penelope, and Clytemnestra), being the husband of a
    widow seems to have offered some claim to the dead king's household.

I swear to you that I never touched your marriage,
never would have wished to, never would have conceived the
    idea.
Indeed may I then perish with no glory, no name,
[cityless, homeless, an exile wandering over the land,]
and may neither sea nor earth receive   1030
my flesh when I'm dead, if I am by nature an evil man.
What it was she feared that she destroyed her life,
I don't know, for it's not right for me to say more.
She who was unable to be virtuous acted virtuously,
but I who was able to be so did not make good use of it.   1035

Chorus Leader
You've spoken an adequate rebuttal of the charge
in offering oaths to the gods, no small pledge.

Theseus
Isn't this man by nature an enchanter and sorcerer,
who is confident that he will master my spirit
with his easy disposition, after he's dishonored the one
    who begot him?   1040

Hippolytus
I marvel very much at the same in you too, father;
for if you were my son and I your father,
I would surely have killed you and would not be punishing
    you with exile,
if you had dared to touch my wife.

Theseus
How like you is what you've said! You will not die in this way,   1045
according to this law you've set up for yourself;
for a quick death is easiest for an unfortunate man.
No, an exile from your fatherland, you will wander

1026: Hippolytus cannot break his oath to the Nurse, but he can swear his
    innocence to his father.
1028: On the theme of reputation in this play, see above on 48 and Essay, p. 69-71.
1034-5: These enigmatic lines, illustrating the shifting semantics of the word
    sophrosyne (**virtue**, more broadly "moderation," on which see above on
    80), offer a concise summary of the play's fundamental dichotomy (from
    Hippolytus' perspective): Phaedra was not (in general) virtuous, but
    performed one act that was chaste (her suicide by which her passions
    were defeated), while Hippolytus, who generally was virtuous, could
    not use this quality to help himself.

over a foreign land and drag out a painful life.
[For these are the wages for an impious man.]   1050

Hippolytus

Oh no! What are you doing? You won't even wait for time
to inform against me, but will drive me from the land?

Theseus

Yes, beyond Pontus and the territories of Atlas,
if I somehow could, so much do I hate you.

Hippolytus

Without examining oath or pledge or the words   1055
of prophets, will you throw me out of the land without a trial?

Theseus

This tablet, without receiving any mantic lot,
accuses you persuasively; and I say good riddance
to the birds flying overhead.

Hippolytus

O gods, why then do I not loose my mouth,   1060
since I am destroyed by you, whom I revere?
No, I will not; I would not in any way persuade those whom I must,
  and I would violate in vain the oaths which I swore.

Theseus

Ah, how your piety will be the death of me!
Get out of your fatherland as quickly as possible.   1065

Hippolytus

Where then will I turn, wretched me? What guest-friend's
house will I go to, when I've been exiled on such a charge?

Theseus

Whoever enjoys bringing in as their guests
those who corrupt their wives and who do wrong while they
  help to guard their houses.

1048-9: Throughout this confrontation with his son, Theseus makes no reference to the curse, only to the exile (see also 973-5). He has no control
over the curse—only the exile.

1060-3: Hippolytus entertains briefly the possibility of speaking the truth
about Phaedra and the Nurse but concludes that it would be unsuccess-
ful and violate his oath as well. Some critics have emphasized that only
the presumed ineffectiveness of violating his oath leads Hippolytus to
keep it, but it should also be noted that when confronted with the reality
of exile he does not in fact violate the sanctity of his oath to the gods.

Hippolytus
> Ah! To the heart; this is near tears,   1070
> *if* I appear evil and seem so to you.

Theseus
> Then you should have wailed and learned at that time,
> when you dared to act outrageously against your father's wife.

Hippolytus
> O house, I wish you could utter a voice for me
> and bear witness whether I am by nature an evil man!   1075

Theseus
> Cleverly you flee to voiceless witnesses;
> but the deed, without speaking, reveals that you are evil.

Hippolytus
> Ah!
> I wish that I could stand opposite and look at myself,
> so that I could cry over how badly I suffer.

Theseus
> *Much* more have you practiced revering yourself   1080
> than showing piety towards your parent, as a just man should.

Hippolytus
> O wretched mother! O bitter birth!
> May none of my friends ever be a bastard!

Theseus
> Take him away, slaves. Haven't you heard me
> for some time declaring his exile?   1085

Hippolytus
> Any one of them who touches me will regret it.
> But you yourself, if that's your desire, thrust me from the land.

Theseus
> I'll do this, if you don't obey my words;
> for no pity for your exile comes upon me.

Hippolytus
> It is fixed, so it seems. Oh wretched me,   1090
> since I know these things, but I don't know how to reveal them!

1071: Appearing evil to his father is painful, but whatever his father may
  believe, Hippolytus does not doubt his own virtue (see 1100-1).
1080-1: Athenians considered reverence towards one's parents the highest
  obligation in the mortal realm.

O daughter of Leto, dearest to me of the divinities,
partner, fellow hunter, I will be exiled
from glorious Athens. So farewell to the city
and land of Erectheus! O plain of Trozen,   1095
you have so much happiness to be young in,
farewell! Looking at you for the last time I address you.
Come, my young companions of this land,
speak to me and escort me from this country,
since you will never see another man   1100
more virtuous, even if this doesn't seem so to my father.

Hippolytus exits down the eisodos *opposite the one by which he entered.*

Theseus exits into the palace, and then the ekkyklema *is wheeled in.*

Chorus:

Strophe A

Greatly does the gods' concern, when it comes to mind,
relieve my distress; and although one conceals his
     understanding in hope,   1105
he falls short of it when looking among the fortunes and deeds of
     mortals.
For things come and go from here and there, and the life of men
     changes,
always wandering.   1110

Antistrophe A

Would that destiny from the gods grant me this in answer to
     my prayers—
fortune with prosperity and a heart untouched by pains;
and may my views be neither exacting nor counterfeit,   1115
but may I share in a life of good fortune, changing my adaptable ways
for the next day always.

1092ff: Hippolytus addresses Artemis' statue, as he had when he first arrived
     on stage.
1102-50. In this song (third *stasimon*) the chorus express their despair about divine
     justice in the wake of Hippolytus' exile and their grief and anger over it.
1105-7: Somewhat opaque in their expression, these lines seem to suggest the
     contrast between an attitude of optimism and the reality of what has
     transpired.
1108-10: Life's inconstancy was commonly expressed by the Greeks.
1117-9: This wish for an adaptable nature echoes the Nurse's attitude at 253ff.
     and contrasts with Hippolytus' at 87.

Strophe B

For no longer do I have a clear mind, and what I see is
  contrary to my hope,   1120
since we saw, we saw the brightest star
of the Greek land rushing to another land
because of his father's anger.   1125
O sands of the city's shore,
o mountain thicket where
he used to kill beasts with swift-footed dogs
in the company of holy Dictynna!   1130

Antistrophe B

No longer will you mount the yoked team of Enetic foals,
holding the course around the Mere as you exercise your horses;
your sleepless music beneath the strings' frame   1135
will cease throughout your father's house.
The resting places of Leto's daughter
will be ungarlanded in the deep verdure;
and by your exile maidens have lost   1140
the bridal contest for your bed.

Epode

But in tears at your misfortune
I will endure
a luckless lot. O wretched mother,
you gave birth in vain! Ah,   1145
I am furious at the gods.
Oh, oh!
Yoked Graces, why do you send this wretched man,
not at all responsible for his ruin,
out of his fatherland, away from this house?   1150

A companion of Hippolytus enters, by the same eisodos *by which
Hippolytus and his attendants departed.*

1138: **Leto's daughter:** Artemis

1141: A reference to Hippolytus' marriage might seem odd, but such a thought
  was conventional and prepares subtly for the cult that will be established
  for Hippolytus at the play's end.

1146: **furious at the gods**: an extremely strong statement.

1148: In art the three **Graces** (Charites), associated with Aphrodite, were
  routinely depicted joined together. The word **yoked** might also suggest
  their role in marriage and procreation.

Chorus Leader
Look, I see here a companion of Hippolytus
with a gloomy look, hastening quickly to the house.

Messenger
Where could I go, women, to find the ruler of this land,
Theseus? If you know, tell me; is he inside this house?   1155

Theseus enters from the palace.

Chorus Leader
Here he is, coming outside the house.

Messenger
Theseus, I carry a report worthy of your
and the citizens' concern, both those who dwell in the city of
    Athens
and those within the boundaries of the Trozenian land.

Theseus
What is it? It can't be that some upsetting misfortune   1160
has befallen the two neighboring cities, can it?

Messenger
Hippolytus is no more, or nearly so;
though precariously balanced in the scales, he still sees the light.

Theseus
At whose hands? It can't be that someone whose wife he
    disgraced forcibly,
as he did his father's, got angry at him, can it?   1165

Messenger
His own team of horses destroyed him,
and the curses from your mouth, which you prayed
to your father, the lord of the sea, against your son.

1151: So-called "messenger scenes" were customary in Greek tragedy. They allowed for the description of off-stage actions (the miraculous bull from the sea was beyond the technical abilities and the aesthetic taste of the Greek theater) and expanded the scope of the drama. This "messenger" (in fact, he conveys news, not a message) is not a neutral party but a companion of Hippolytus. This explains his ability to report in vivid details what happened and gives another opportunity for someone to declare Hippolytus' innocence.

1161: **two neighboring cities**: Athens and Trozen, linked more politically than geographically.

Theseus
 O gods and Poseidon, how you truly are my father after all,
 since you've listened to my curses!   1170
 How did he perish? Tell me, in what way did the club of Justice
 strike him after he disgraced me?

Messenger
 We were near the wave-beaten shore,
 in tears as we groomed the horses' coats
 with currycombs; for a messenger had come telling us 1175
 that Hippolytus could no longer dwell in this land,
 since he had been banished by you to a wretched exile.
 And he came to us at the shore
 in the same strain of tears, and a countless assembly of friends
 <and> age-mates was walking along behind him. 1180
 Finally he ceased from his groans and said:
 "Why do I carry on this way in my grief? My father's words must
  be obeyed.
 Harness the yoke-bearing horses to the chariot,
 servants, for this is no longer my city."
  And then from that point every man hurried,   1185
 and faster than one could say it, we had readied
 the horses and set them right by our master.
 He seized the reins from the rail with his hands,
 fitting his feet right into the footstalls.
 And first he opened his palms upwards and said to the gods, 1190
 "Zeus, may I be no more, if I am by nature an evil man;
 but may my father perceive how he dishonors me,
 either when I am dead or while I still see the light."
 At that moment, taking the goad into his hands he began to lay it
 upon the horses all at the same time; and we attendants were
  following   1195
 our master below the chariot near the bridle,
 along the road that goes straight to Argos and Epidaurus.

1169: Like all mortal children of gods, Theseus could not be sure of his paternity. Now, the curses' prove to him that Poseidon is his father. The
  confirmation of this paternity stands out after the brutal confrontation
  between father and son in the previous scene.
1190: This was the habitual gesture for praying to the gods of the upper air.
1197: **Argos and Epidaurus**: Cities to the west and northwest respectively of
  Trozen.

And when we were coming into the desolate territory,
there is a headland beyond this land,
lying towards what is by then the Saronic Gulf.   1200
From there an echo from the earth, like Zeus' thunder,
let forth a deep roar, hair-raising to hear;
the horses stood their heads and ears straight
towards the heavens, and we were very afraid
about where in the world the voice came from. And looking   1205
towards the sea-loud coast we saw a supernatural
wave fixed towards the heavens, so that my eye
was robbed of the sight of the coast of Sciron,
and it was covering the Isthmus and the rock of Asclepius.
And then swollen and foaming with   1210
froth all around it, with a blast from the sea
it advanced toward the shore where the four-horse chariot was.
And along with its very swell and triple crest
the wave spewed forth a bull, a savage monster.
The whole land was filled with its voice   1215
and was giving a hair-raising roar in reply, and the sight of it
appeared greater than we who were looking on could absorb.
    And at once a terrible panic fell upon the horses;
my master, who was very familiar
with the ways of horses, snatched the reins in his hands   1220
and he pulled them, the way a sailor does an oar,
leaning his body backwards on the reins.
But biting on the fire-forged bits with their jaws,
they carried him against his will, heeding neither the helmsman's
    hand nor the harness nor the well-made chariot.   1225
And whenever, holding the tiller,
he steered their course toward the soft ground,
the bull would appear in front to turn them back,

1198: **desolate territory**: In Greek myth, miraculous phenomena typically
    occur in isolated areas.
1209: **Isthmus**: of Corinth, near which the **rock of Asclepius** (of unknown
    precise location) presumably stood.
1214: **bull**: The bull was associated with Poseidon and could represent un-
    tamed masculinity. Bulls also played a role in Phaedra's and Theseus'
    family histories; see Introduction, p. xxii.
1218ff.: The master horseman, Hippolytus is ruined by his horses, just as,
    e.g., the hunter Actaeon was killed by his hunting dogs.

and drive the four-horse team mad with fear;
and whenever with their maddened minds they rushed towards
   the rocks   1230
it would follow nearby in silence alongside the rail
until it finally tripped up and overturned
the chariot, smashing the wheel's rim against the rock.
Everything was mixed together: the wheels' hubs
and the axles' pins were leaping up,   1235
and the wretch himself, bound up in the reins'
inextricable bond, was being dragged,
smashing his own head against the rocks
and shattering his flesh, and shouting out in a way that was
   terrible to hear:
"Stop, you who were reared in my stables,   1240
don't wipe me out! Oh my father's wretched curse!
Who wishes to come and save the best of men?"
And many of us who wished to do so were left behind
with our slower pace. And, freed from the bonds,
the cut leather reins—I don't know how—   1245
he fell still breathing a *little* life;
and the horses and the disastrous monstrous bull
disappeared—I don't know where in the rugged land.
   I'm only a slave in your house, lord,
but I will never be able to do this,   1250
to believe that your son is evil,
not even if the entire race of women should be hanged,
and someone should fill the pine forest on Ida
with writing; for I know that he is good.
Chorus Leader
Ah, a misfortune of new ills is accomplished,   1255
and there is no escape from destiny and necessity.
Theseus
Because of my hatred of the man who has suffered this,
I took delight in these words; but now feeling a sense of shame

1241: It is not clear how Hippolytus learned of his father's curse, but it is not
   implausible that he might have heard of it. In any case, such matters did
   not commonly trouble ancient playwrights.
1253: **Ida:** A reference to one of two wooded mountains, most likely the one
   near Troy, famous from Homer.

before the gods and him, because he is my son,
I neither take delight in these ills nor am I distressed at them. 1260

Messenger

What now? Bring him here, or what should
we do with the wretched one to satisfy your will?
Think about it; but if you take my counsel,
you will not be savage towards your son in his misfortune.

Theseus

Bring him here, so that I can see him before my eyes   1265
and refute with arguments and the misfortunes from the gods
the one who denied that he defiled my bed.

*Hippolytus' companion exits down th*e eisodos *by which he entered.*

Chorus

You lead the unbending mind of gods and of mortals captive,
Cypris, and along with you is
the one with many-colored wings, encompassing them   1270
with his very swift wing;
Eros flies over the earth
and over the sweet-echoing briny sea,
and he bewitches anyone whose maddened heart
he rushes against, winged and gold-shining—   1275
the young of the mountains and those of the sea,
whatever the earth nourishes
and the blazing sun looks upon,
and men; over all of these, Cypris,   1280
you alone hold sway in royal power.

Artemis enters on high.

1268-81: The chorus' final song (fourth *stasimon*) is very short, a hymn to the
power of Cypris and Eros, in the wake of what has transpired. This song
will be followed immediately by Artemis' arrival. Just as in the play's
beginning Aphrodite's exit was followed by a song to Artemis, here
near the play's conclusion a song to Aphrodite immediately precedes
Artemis' appearance.

1270: **the one with many-colored wings**: Eros.

1281: *Artemis enters on high.* Divine epiphanies were part of Greek literature
and especially favored by Euripides at the end of his plays. Here the
goddess informs the characters of information they could not have known
otherwise, helps to effect the reconciliation of father and son, predicts
the future, and establishes a cult for Hippolytus. Artemis would have
appeared on the roof of the *skene*, brought there by the *mechane*, a crane-

Artemis
> You, the noble-born son of Aegeus,
> I command you to listen:
> I, the daughter of Leto, Artemis, address you.   1285
> Why, wretched Theseus, do you take delight in this,
> killing your son impiously,
> when you were persuaded of unclear things by your wife's
> lying words? But it was a clear ruin you got.
> Why then do you not in your disgrace hide in Tartarus,   1290
> or change to a winged life above
> and lift your foot out of this pain? For you have no share
> of life among good men.   1295
>   Listen, Theseus, to the state of your ills.
> And yet I'll accomplish nothing, except to pain you.
> But I came for this: to reveal your son's mind
> as just, so that he may die with a good reputation,
> and your wife's frenzied lust or, in a way,   1300
> nobility. For stung by the goads
> of the goddess most hateful to us who take delight in virginity,
> she fell in love with your son;
> and trying to overcome Cypris with her reason
> she was destroyed, against her will, by the contrivances of her
>   Nurse,   1305
> who, after she obtained his oath, revealed the sickness to your son.
> And he, as was in fact just, did not go along
> with these words, nor in turn, since he is pious by birth,
> did he retract the pledge of his oath when he was abused by you.
> And she, in fear that she would be found out,   1310
> wrote lying letters and destroyed
> your son by her tricks, but still she persuaded you.

---

like device developed for this purpose. Her position, literal and meta-
phoric, contrasts sharply with the mortals who suffer at ground level.
Initially she speaks in anapests (a meter suggesting greater formality); at
1296 she converts to standard iambic meter.

1290: **Tartarus**: Serves as another name for Hades, the underworld.

1297ff. Like Phaedra, Artemis is concerned both with preserving a good
reputation (Hippolytus') and vengeance.

1300-1: **frenzied lust or . . . nobility**: This alternative explanation juxtaposes
two aspects of Phaedra's situation—the divinely caused passion for her
stepson and her nobility in combating it.

Theseus
Ah!

Artemis
Does this story sting you, Theseus? Be still,
so that you may hear what happened next and groan more.
Do you know that you had three sure curses from your
father? 1315
You took one of these, o you most evil one,
to use against your son, when you could have used it against an
enemy.
Now your father from the sea, being well disposed towards you,
gave only what he had to, since he had agreed.
But you appear evil in both his eyes and mine, 1320
since you waited for neither proof nor the voice
of prophets, didn't bring things to the test, didn't allow
long time to inquire; but sooner than you should have,
you hurled curses against your son and killed him.

Theseus
Mistress, may I perish!

Artemis
You did terrible things, but even so 1325
it is still possible for you to obtain forgiveness even of them;
for Cypris wanted these things to happen,
sating her desire. This is the custom of the gods:
no one is willing to oppose the desire
of whoever wants something, but we always stand aloof. 1330
For—know this well—if I hadn't feared Zeus
I would never have come to this degree of disgrace,
to allow the dearest to me of all mortals
to die. But first of all your not knowing
frees your error from wickedness; 1335
and then your wife in dying did away with
the refutation of her words, so that she persuaded your mind.

1326: Artemis does not say that she will forgive Theseus, only that he might
obtain forgiveness. Forgiveness is not a common attribute of Greek
gods.
1328-30: Artemis states as principle what is implicit in much of Greek literature—the gods' non-intervention, even to help their favorites.
1334-5: Theseus' ignorance makes him less culpable, but no less responsible.

These evils then have burst upon you especially,
but it is painful for me too; for the gods do not enjoy it
when the pious die, but we destroy   1340
the base along with their children and houses.

*Hippolytus enters supported by attendants, by the same eisodos by which
he left.*

Chorus Leader
Look, here the wretched one approaches,
his youthful flesh and blond head
mangled. Oh pain for the house,
what a double grief has been brought to pass for the house,   1345
seizing it by the gods' will!

Hippolytus
Ah, ah!
I am wretched! I've been mangled
by unjust divine pronouncements from an unjust father.
I am ruined, wretched me, woe is me!   1350
Pains shoot through my head,
and a spasm throbs in my brain.
Stop, let me rest my worn-out body.
Ah, ah!
O hateful team of horses,
nourished at my hand,   1355
you've destroyed me,
you've killed me.
Ah, ah! By the gods, gently
hold on to my wounded flesh with your hands, servants.
Who stands by my side on the right?   1360
Lift me properly, move me carefully,
ill-starred and accursed
because of my father's errors. Zeus, Zeus, do you see this?
Here I am, the reverent and god-revering,

1339-40: By echoing the traditional imprecation against oath-breakers, this
phrase invites an implicit comparison with Hippolytus, who did not
break his oath.

1341: In his arrival, weak and near death and accompanied by attendants,
Hippolytus echoes Phaedra's first appearance. Hippolytus' self-lamen-
tation, cries of innocence and prayer for death are all in lyric meters, the
excited rhythms matching the intensity of his words and situation.

here I am, the one who surpassed everyone in virtue,   1365
I'm walking into a death clear before my eyes, having utterly
lost my life
and toiled in vain
performing labors of piety for men.
Ah, ah!   1370
Even now pain, pain comes over me—
let go of wretched me!—
and now may death the healer come to me!
Add death to my pain, death for me the unfortunate.
I desire a two-edged weapon,   1375
to rend me asunder and put
my life to sleep.
Oh my father's wretched curse!
A blood-tainted inherited evil
of long-ago ancestors   1380
breaks its bounds,
and does not stay in place,
and has come upon me—why in the world me,
who am completely blameless of evils?
Woe is me, woe!
What can I say? How can I rid   1385
my life
of this suffering and make it painless?
Would that the black-as-night
compulsion of Hades might lay me,
the ill-starred, to sleep!

Chorus Leader
O wretched one, what a misfortune you've been yoked to;
your nobility of mind destroyed you.   1390

Hippolytus
Ah!
Oh divine fragrance. Even in my troubles
I recognized you and my body was lightened.
The goddess Artemis is in this place.

Artemis
O wretched one, she is, the dearest to you of the gods.

1379-83: See above on 819.

Hippolytus

Do you see me, mistress, how wretched I am?   1395

Artemis

I see you; but it is not right for me to shed a tear from my eyes.

Hippolytus

You don't have your huntsman or your attendant.

Artemis

No; but you who are dear to me are dying.

Hippolytus

Or your horseman or the guardian of your statues.

Artemis

No, for Cypris, the wicked one, planned it this way.   1400

Hippolytus

Ah! I understand what divinity has destroyed me.

Artemis

She found fault with your homage, and she was vexed at your
    virtue.

Hippolytus

Single-handedly she destroyed the three of us, I realize.

Artemis

Yes, your father, and you, and his wife, third.

Hippolytus

I groan then also for my father's bad fortunes.   1405

Artemis

He was completely deceived by the divinity's plans.

Hippolytus

O father, most wretched because of your misfortune!

Theseus

I am ruined, child, and I have no pleasure in life.

Hippolytus

I groan for you more than me at this error.

1396: The gods keep their distance from mortals' suffering; see also 1437-8.

1402: Artemis' view of Aphrodite's motivation is, predictably, somewhat
    different from the latter's stated reasons in her prologue speech.

1405ff. From here on, Hippolytus, despite his ruin at his father's hands,
    expresses concern and sympathy for him.

Theseus
If only I could become a corpse instead of you, child!   1410
Hippolytus
Oh the bitter gifts of your father Poseidon!
Theseus
Would that they had never come to my lips!
Hippolytus
What?! You surely would have killed me, so angry were you then.
Theseus
Yes, we were tripped up in our judgment by the gods.
Hippolytus
Ah! Would that the race of mortals could be a curse on
        the gods.   1415
Artemis
Let it be. For not even under the darkness of earth
will the anger of the goddess Cypris that stems from her
 desire rush down against your body unavenged,
thanks to your piety and noble mind.
For I will take vengeance by my hand   1420
with these inescapable arrows on another, one of hers.
whatever mortal is her very dearest,
    But to you, o miserable one, in return for these ills,
I will give the greatest honors in the city
of Trozen: unyoked maidens before marriage   1425
will cut off locks of their hair for you, who over a long time
will enjoy the fruits of their tears' deepest mourning.
Always the maidens will be inspired to sing songs
about you, and Phaedra's love for you will not

1415: Remarkably, this curse is made against the gods. Cf. the chorus' words at 1146.

1416ff.: Just as Aphrodite took vengeance on Hippolytus, Artemis will take vengeance on one of Aphrodite's favorites, not named here but almost certainly Adonis, who died gored by a boar while hunting. **Unavenged . . . take vengeance**: from the same verbal root and part of the same matrix of honor/payment; cf. Aphrodite's words at 8 and 21.

1424ff. Artemis promises a cult for Hippolytus, in which he will be honored in death by Trozenian maidens, who will offer him locks of their hair before their marriage. Hippolytus, who rejected sex and marriage during his life, will be venerated by young women before their marriage. On the historical cult alluded to here, see Introduction, p. xxi.

fall away nameless and be kept silent. 1430
But you, o child of aged Aegeus, take
your son in your arms and embrace him.
For in ignorance you killed him, and it is likely
that mortals err greatly when the gods bring it about.
And I urge you not to hate your father, 1435
Hippolytus; for you have your fate with which you were
    destroyed.
And so farewell; it is not right for me to see the dead
nor to defile my sight with final breaths.
And I see that you are now near this evil.

Artemis exits.

Hippolytus
Farewell to you too as you go, blessed maiden; 1440
easily you leave a long companionship.
I dissolve the strife with my father, since you wish it;
for also before I obeyed your words.
Ah, darkness now comes down upon my eyes.
Hold on to me, father, and straighten my body. 1445

Theseus
Ah! Child, what are you doing to me, the ill-starred?

Hippolytus
I'm dead, and already I see the gates of the dead.

Theseus
Leaving my hand impure?

Hippolytus
No, since I free you from this bloodshed.

Theseus
What are you saying? You're acquitting me of blood? 1450

Hippolytus
I call to witness Artemis who subdues with arrows.

Theseus
O dearest one, how noble you are revealed to your father.

1441: This line has been interpreted as reflecting various attitudes—from
    resentment to pious resignation. At the very least it underscores the
    profound separation between gods and mortals. The play concludes
    with the mortal players only.

Hippolytus

O farewell to you, too, father, I bid you a long farewell.

Theseus

Ah, for your pious and noble mind!

Hippolytus

Pray that you have legitimate sons such as me.   1455

Theseus

Don't now leave me, child, but endure!

Hippolytus

My enduring's over; I'm dead, father.

Cover my face with my robes as quickly as possible.

Theseus

Famous Athens and the boundaries of Pallas,

what a man you will lack! Oh wretched me,   1460

how much, Cypris,will I remember your evils!

Theseus exits into the palace and attendants carry in Hippolytus' corpse.

Chorus

This grief to be shared by all the citizens

came unexpectedly.

There will be a splashing of many tears;

for sorrowful tales about the great   1465

hold greater sway.

The chorus exit down the eisodos *by which they arrived.*

1462-6. All of Euripides' plays end with a choral coda, providing formal closure to the drama, not that different from the "THE END" that appears at the conclusion of many films.

The *Hippolytus*: An Interpretation

No one has ever challenged the assessment of the *Hippolytus* pronounced by Aristophanes of Byzantium—"this play is among the best." It displays some of Euripides' finest poetry and a fascinating portrayal of many of life's basic emotions and concerns—passion, honor, family, reputation, virtue, and death. Working with traditional material, the playwright crafted a nuanced and intricate exploration of these issues, embedding them within a powerful dramatic structure. In this essay, I look at various aspects of the drama, trying to tease out some of the richness of its themes, patterns, and meanings.

PLOT, STRUCTURE, AND DESIGN

While the fundamental story of the play conforms to the motif of "Potiphar's Wife," another story pattern is grafted onto this one, that of revenge. What drives this play is not simply Phaedra's passion for Hippolytus, but also Aphrodite's revenge against him. The two patterns are clearly joined in Aphrodite's prologue speech when she explains that she will punish Hippolytus by having his stepmother fall in love with him. Many have observed that the actions of the play are credible without the divinities' direct participation—the destructive force of illicit passion is readily understandable. But with their active involvement it is a very different drama. Phaedra's passion becomes in a sense secondary; Hippolytus' violent rejection is seen as a rebuff not only of his stepmother, but of a divinity; and human actions are subject to a different kind of moral calculus. And, of course, dramatic irony permeates the whole play to a degree that would be impossible without Aphrodite's speech explaining her intervention. It is possible that the deities were added directly to this play as part of the decision to rewrite the earlier one; that is, the role of Aphrodite was introduced to mitigate Phaedra's culpability. Whatever the motivation, such a prologue alters the prism through which we view the play. The added dimension of the divine does not displace the mortal one but rather complicates it.

The formal excellence of *Hippolytus* is universally accepted. Part of that excellence is its artful structure, one which, while dealing with two disparate motifs, joins them in a balanced whole. The play seems to fall into two roughly even halves, the first (1-775) devoted chiefly, although not exclusively, to Phaedra (and Hippolytus), the second (776-1466), chiefly to Hippolytus (and Theseus). With the conclusion of the second stasimon (775), Phaedra is dead, her brave fight against her passion and for her good name over, and the action turns to Hippolytus' combat against the false charge of rape and for his reputation before his father's eyes. A long episode of roughly equal length dominates each of the play's halves (170-524 [355 lines] and 776-1101 [326 lines, or, with some likely deletions, 322]). In the first one, the Nurse extracts from a silent and reluctant Phaedra the truth about her sexual passion for Hippolytus and engages her in debate about it. In the second, Theseus believes Phaedra's lying note about Hippolytus' (alleged) sexual violation of his wife and then, after condemning him, debates with Hippolytus about this charge (902-1101).

The play offers a "divine frame:" Artemis' appearance at the end balances Aphrodite's at the beginning. Although Euripides very frequently introduced gods into the beginnings and ends of his dramas, this is only one of three plays (*Ion* and *Bacchae* being the other two) in which gods appear both at the beginning and at the end. While these two goddesses stand on opposite sides (against and for Hippolytus), and can be read symbolically as representing different aspects of the world (e.g., sexuality and chastity), they have much in common in their motives and language, and these similarities underscore the play's symmetrical structure. A brief astrophic song to Artemis follows immediately Aphrodite's departure; a brief astrophic song to Aphrodite precedes Artemis' entrance.

Other structural and visual parallels give shape to the drama. When Phaedra first arrives on stage, she is half-dead, carried by attendants and giving lyric expression to her woes. Later in the play Hippolytus arrives half-dead, supported by attendants and speaking initially in lyrics. Upon Phaedra's arrival, the chorus and Nurse in ignorance ask about the cause of her plight. When Hippolytus returns to the stage (901), he is ignorant of and inquires about Theseus' situation. Two acts of supplication, from sequential scenes, also provide parallel structures. Phaedra's refusal to tell her Nurse what afflicts her is met with the extreme (and successful) act of supplication, which ultimately breaks Phaedra's silence. In the following scene, the Nurse attempts another act of supplication, this time of Hippolytus, to obtain not his speech, but his silence. This time, the supplication itself fails (although a previously extracted oath holds).

HUMAN CHARACTERS AND THE GODS

Few among the surviving Greek tragedies have attracted as much interest in their characters as *Hippolytus*. The chaste and tortured Phaedra, the religiously dedicated and proud Hippolytus have been the subject of many studies. Theseus and the Nurse do not demand the same sort of attention, but interestingly among these four characters there is no huge difference in the number of lines spoken by each. While this play is not primarily a psychological drama, the characters are drawn carefully, in relation both to each other and to the gods.

Aphrodite offers the first portrait of Hippolytus: he is an arrogant young man who should be punished for his contempt for her world. Hippolytus presents himself as a devoted follower of Artemis. His opening address to her (73-87) reflects a pious and committed soul. Yet these same words also reflect an exclusivity and narrowness. These traits, already observed by Aphrodite, are revealed again in the scene between Hippolytus and his servant, as he expresses his reservations about gods "worshipped at night" (106) and his disrespect for Aphrodite (113). His response to the Nurse's proposition is extraordinary, leading him not only to condemn all women, but even to wish for a world in which there were no women at all (616-24). Yet in this furious attack, he vows to maintain his oath of silence, a vow that he will keep, even at the cost of his own life. His fury, moreover, makes some sense in the context of the Nurse's falsely asserting that her mistress seeks a sexual union with him. Those who fault Hippolytus for his outrageous conduct here also condemn what they see as his frigid and self-righteous behavior towards his father later on and his proud self-proclamations of virtue then and in the concluding scene. Hippolytus has, to be sure, no small opinion of himself and follows a rigid and exclusive adherence to one divinity, but he also possesses an impressive piety and religious devotion. His pious devotion and his ruin are part of the same cloth (see 1402).

Phaedra in this play is no longer the brazen and intemperate woman of *Hippolytus I*, but rather is presented as virtuous and intent on doing the right thing. Her virtue is proclaimed by Aphrodite (47-8) and Artemis (1300-6) alike; the Nurse, at the very moment when she learns of her mistress' passion for Hippolytus, includes her among the chaste (358-9); and even Hippolytus has grudging admiration for her (1034-5). The early part of the play especially shows her deep struggle against her passion and her valiant attempts to retain her virtue.

A different Phaedra requires a different Hippolytus; the new Phaedra of the second *Hippolytus* needs a more subtle and ambiguous figure to play against. Hippolytus is now presented as one in comparison to whom the suffering Phaedra appears the more sympathetic, and against whom her false accusations seem less reprehensible. Writing the lying tablet cannot—and should not—be dismissed; it is (at least in part) vindictive and destructive. But the characterization of Hippolytus leavens judgment against Phaedra. Several other factors also militate against viewing her behavior in an unfavorable light: Aphrodite, a powerful and external force, is seen as the cause of her passion; Phaedra herself has tried greatly to master this illicit desire; the Nurse, not Phaedra, brings about her confession of this desire and the conveying of it to Hippolytus. Another important aspect is Phaedra's Cretan past. Her mother Pasiphaë was afflicted with passion for a bull, her sister is said to be ill-fated in love, and throughout the play we are reminded of this Cretan background (esp. 337-41, and cf. 372, 719 and 752ff.). In fighting against her passion, Phaedra is trying to overcome her family lineage, while also contrasting with her literary predecessor of the earlier play.

Conveniently absent from the first part of the play, Theseus, on his return, immediately following Phaedra's death, is confronted with his wife's corpse and lying note. He responds with grief and outrage, condemning his son and punishing him with a curse and exile. Like Hippolytus, Theseus himself comes from an illegitimate union (between Aethra and Aegeus—or Poseidon), and he is unsure of his paternity. (For him the efficacy of the curse establishes Poseidon as his father, 1169-70.) His reaction is rash, as the chorus (891-2), Hippolytus (1051-2) and Artemis (1321-4) all claim. But this rashness is needed for the plot and is in keeping with his character as a man of action. At the end of the play, he reveals his remorse and his eagerness to be reconciled with his son.

Euripides, famed for "domesticating" tragedy, nowhere else developed so fully a non-aristocratic character like Phaedra's Nurse. She is essential not only as a catalyst for the plot (without her, Phaedra would die and Aphrodite's revenge fizzle), but also in serving as an interlocutor and foil for Phaedra. Phaedra's passion could be explored in a monologue (by Phaedra) only so far; the Nurse, with her persistent questions, forceful supplication, and opposing views, allows for an extended examination of it. She contrasts with Phaedra at almost every turn. She is ignorant when Phaedra is tormented by knowledge of her passion; she is eager for speech when Phaedra is for silence; she is stunned while Phaedra talks; she wants action while Phaedra wants a good name; she wants Phaedra's life when Phaedra has already chosen death. Her chief motivating force is her interest in Phaedra's life. Unlike Phaedra, however, she has no concern for other moral standards and judges things only with a pragmatist's interest in results

(700-1). Her role in the plot should not be undervalued, but to think of her as an agent of Aphrodite is to overstate the case and to misread the gods' role in the drama.

The goddesses, appearing at the play's beginning and end, have much to do with its outcome, but, as often in Greek literature, they rely very much on human behavior to effect it. Aphrodite causes Phaedra to fall in love with her stepson, but she does not compel her response to this passion or the other responses that ripple from it. She predicts most of the major events of the play, but that is not the same as causing them. Phaedra, the Nurse, Hippolytus, and Theseus all respond as autonomous individuals under the circumstances created by the divinity. It is true that vital decisions are made under misconceptions and in ignorance, but these are made by the mortals, not the gods. Not only Aphrodite, but many mortals contribute to the play's tragic outcome. Phaedra's intense desire for her good name; the Nurse's relaying Phaedra's passion to Hippolytus; Hippolytus' own savage response; Theseus' rashness in punishing his son—these all contribute to Hippolytus' and Phaedra's deaths and Theseus' desolation. Poseidon, to be sure, also contributes by sending the bull from the sea, but, as Artemis says (1318-9), he did only what he had to, fulfilling one of the prayers he promised to Theseus, and Hippolytus is traveling along the shore, where the bull attacks, because he has been exiled by Theseus. Artemis, in explaining matters to Theseus and Hippolytus, lays the primary blame on her fellow divinity (1301-3, 1325-8, 1400, 1416-22), but she also finds fault with Phaedra (1310-2), the Nurse (1305-6), and especially Theseus (1285-95, 1297, 1316-7, 1321-4, 1325). There is plenty of blame to go around.

The gods' power is clear; the rightness of it is not. Hippolytus' servant remarks that gods should be wiser than mortals and forgive someone like Hippolytus (114-20). There is no reason to regard this as privileged discourse, the "voice of the poet," but it does offer the suggestion that Aphrodite's planned punishment is excessive, at least from a mortal perspective. Artemis, in sharing many traits with Aphrodite, is open to the same criticisms. She could not prevent Aphrodite's vengeance, but will in return exact vengeance from a mortal, one of Aphrodite's favorites (1420-2). The play's violence, triggered by a goddess's vengeance, will thus continue against another mortal. Artemis does assist in reconciling father and son (1435), but she does not stay with Hippolytus as he dies (1437-8). Hippolytus' response, "Easily you leave a long companionship" (1441) is difficult to interpret neutrally. His entire relationship with Artemis, although special, is asymmetrical: he cannot see her (85-6; cf. 1391-2), and her concern for him has real limits. The divine frame is only partial. Artemis is gone before the play ends. Its final moments show Theseus embracing his son, Hippolytus forgiving his father. Aphrodite's evils will not be forgotten (1461), but neither will the human actions that dominate the drama. The concluding choral tag (1462-6) ignores the gods and focuses entirely on the grief for Hippolytus and the fame born of great men.

SPEECH, SILENCE, AND DECEPTION

It has long been recognized that this play is deeply concerned with speech, silence, and their consequences. Words for speech and silence permeate the play, and each character makes important decisions about speech and silence; the consequences of these decisions give the drama much of its shape. The importance of silence is announced in Aphrodite's prologue when she explains that Phaedra is dying in silence (40). Phaedra breaks this silence in a series of lyric outbursts (198ff.), only to return to silence in shame at what she has said (244). The Nurse then deliberately seeks to break through this silence, succeeding finally through supplication, and only gradually and partially does Phaedra bring herself to speak out about her passion. Hearing of this passion functionally silences the Nurse, while Phaedra gives a *rhesis* in which she explains that her first effort at combating her passion was silence and concealment (394). Phaedra is soon afraid that the Nurse will succeed in using "overly fine words" (487) that prove destructive; she wants the Nurse to be silent (498-9). The Nurse will not be silent and reveals to Hippolytus her mistress's desire for him. This is the first of several important misrepresentations in the play. The Nurse, acting from a brand of pragmatism and taking advantage of many verbal ambiguities (see 486-524n.), presents Phaedra as other than she wants—or intends—to be. Without this misrepresentation the play's disastrous actions would not proceed. But the resourceful Nurse does, in advance of making her case to Hippolytus, secure from him an oath of silence. Although the young man will implicitly threaten to break this oath (612), he will ultimately abide by it and keep silent because of his piety. Shocked, however, by the Nurse's proposal, he issues a long and violent speech against women, which includes the wish that women had only *voiceless* beasts as attendants (646). This speech proves destructive, since in response to it Phaedra fears that he will in fact reveal her passion (689-92) and wants to punish him for his arrogance (728-31). The chorus's complicity in her plotting is secured by their own oath of silence (710-4). However one imagines Phaedra's location during Hippolytus' speech (see 600n.), the two main characters never address one another in this play of many miscommunications.

In going to her death, Phaedra explains that she needs "new words" (688). These words prove to be the written tablet she leaves for Theseus in which she falsely accuses Hippolytus of rape. This tablet "speaks" for her and in Theseus' description it is repeatedly personified (see 856n.). Phaedra has created a false but persuasive representation of Hippolytus, to which Theseus responds with two speech acts of his own: a curse on his son (to be fulfilled by Poseidon) and a proclamation of exile. When Hippolytus returns to the stage, Theseus is initially silent and Hippolytus tries to elicit speech from him (911), but at the end of this scene it is Hippolytus who becomes silent because of his oath (1060-3), and wishes for mute witnesses to his character (1074-5). Also in this scene Theseus wishes for a world in which everyone would have two voices, one of which could refute the lying one (928-31). Words that break through the lies and misrepresentations come from Artemis, who explains Aphrodite's role, Phaedra's lying words, and the Nurse's tricks, while condemning Theseus' own hasty actions. Two important speech acts remain, one promised, the other enacted. Hippolytus will be commemorated in a cult in which his name will not pass into oblivion and Phaedra's passion for him will not grow silent (1429-30). Finally, Hippolytus forgives his father in words that, unlike most in the play, effect reconciliation and not destruction.

REPUTATION, SHAME, AND HONOR

Phaedra's desire for a good reputation (*eukleia*) ranks high among her many motivations. In sharp contrast to her counterpart in *Hippolytus I*, this Phaedra is determined to act virtuously, to preserve her good name at all costs. It is important to remember that fifth-century Athens was still predominantly a "shame culture," that is, one in which excellence and its opposite were measured by external standards and one's worth was not easily distinguished from one's reputation. Accordingly, one often finds expressions such as "may I not be seen doing X" where we might say "may I not do X." In her prologue, Aphrodite predicts that even in death Phaedra will have a good reputation (47). Phaedra herself emphasizes the importance of this reputation explicitly by using the word *euklees* (the adjectival form of *eukleia*) and its opposite several times of herself and her children. When the play opens she has already determined to take her own life, knowing that illicit passion brought a bad reputation (405) and being unwilling to compromise her children's good reputation coming from their mother (419-23); after the Nurse's revelation to Hippolytus, Phaedra fears that she will no longer die with such a reputation (687-8); but then she finds a remedy to ensure her children's good name after all (717). The chorus confirms the importance of her good name in the song that follows her exit to her death (772-3). Hippolytus, when he is faced with exile, prays that he die without fame (1028) if he is evil, and Artemis, at the end of the play, acknowledges Phaedra's "nobility" (1301), but explains that she has come so that Hippolytus may die in good repute (1299).

In order to ensure her good reputation, Phaedra seeks to avoid anything that might cause disgrace. She cannot bear the thought of disgracing her husband (420, 720-1) or her Cretan home (719). In these cases the word used for "disgrace" is the verb *aischuno* or its related adjective. After expressing her desire for the mountains and horses, she checks herself out of shame at her words (244). The word used to express shame here is *aidos*. *Aidos*, prominent in the play, refers to a complex set of emotions which include the feeling that inhibits one from improper action; it is "that which renders one sensitive to the general values of society and inhibits departure from them."[1] In part, it keeps one from conduct that would jeopardize one's good name. It is also what one feels having committed such action; thus it suggests "shame" as well as "reverence, respect." At the crucial juncture where Phaedra yields to the Nurse's supplication, she explains, "I respect [feel *aidos* before] your supplication" (335). Later, after this respect for the Nurse's supplication leads to what she feels will be certain disgrace, she kills herself, feeling, the chorus imagine, shame (*aidos*) at her misfortune (772). *Aidos* is also significantly placed in her major speech explaining the motives of her actions (385-6). For Hippolytus, a personified *aidos* tends his exclusive, inviolate meadow (78). It is the feeling that operates in those he would consider his friends (998). While the word appears in connection with Theseus only in explaining his curtailed joy at his son's death (1258), he implicitly refers to this concept when he imagines that if he does not punish his son he will seem inferior in the eyes of the brigands he has already punished (976-80).

The reference to another's gaze, fundamental to the dynamics of a "shame culture," appears several times in this play. It is reflected in the words of all three main characters: Phaedra wonders how adulterers can look their husbands in the eye (415-6), and explains that she will never come before Theseus after doing disgraceful deeds (721); Hippolytus threatens that when he returns he will observe how Phaedra and her Nurse can look at Theseus (661-2); Theseus commands Hippolytus to show his face to his father (946-7), and hopes to refute his son face to face (1265).

Honor forms another part of this matrix. Honor is an outward manifestation of one's worth, and gods and mortals display a keen interest in it. Aphrodite in her prologue explains the role of honor as a general

---

1 D. Cairns, *Aidos*, 154.

principle—gods like being honored (8). Hippolytus honors Artemis (16; cf. 55), not Aphrodite, who will punish Hippolytus for her perceived lack of it from him (21). The word for "punish" which Aphrodite uses at 21 is etymologically related to words for "honor" (the root is *tim-*), punishment being a way of establishing or protecting one's worth, one's honor. Hippolytus' refusal to honor Aphrodite lies at the center of his tragedy, and this refusal is underscored in his exchange with his servant (88ff., esp. 107 and 104) and confirmed by Artemis (1402). Phaedra's intended suicide will, she feels, bring her honor (329). And in writing the lying tablet she will punish Hippolytus (see esp. 728-31, although no word from the root *tim-* is used). Theseus mocks Hippolytus' (seemingly) feigned honoring of mystic texts (954). After learning of Hippolytus' destruction, the chorus sing of Aphrodite's extraordinary "power" (1281), another sense of the word *time*. At the end of the play Artemis declares that Aphrodite's anger against her favorite will not be "unavenged" (*atimoi*, 1417), but, like Aphrodite, she will herself both take vengeance (*timoresomai*, 1422; cf. 21) and establish a Trozenian cult in which Hippolytus will receive honors (*timai*, 1424).

SOPHROSUNE

No word is more fundamental to any Greek play than *sophrosune* is to this one, and in no other play do words from this root appear so often (18 times—*Bacchae* with 12 occurrences is the next highest). In its most radical sense the word means "safe-mindedness," the quality which allows one to act sensibly. In Plato's *Symposium* (196c) it is defined by Agathon as "being in control of pleasures and desires," while Antiphon (frag. 59 D-K) sees its essence in not merely not desiring what is evil, but in overcoming temptation. Its semantic sphere came to include various senses, including the several found in this play—good sense, self-control, sexual self-control, i.e., chastity, and virtue (in general).[2] In the play Hippolytus himself claims several times that no one is more *sophron* (the adjective of the noun) than he (995, 1100, 1365), condemns women who are not *sophron* (see esp. 667), wishes that his being *sophron* could persuade his father of his innocence (1007), and realizes that Phaedra was in some sense better able to use *sophrosune* than he (1034-5 and note). He also defends himself to his father with an argument about those who are, like him, *sophron* (1013), while Artemis defends him as being *sophron* (1402). Phaedra tries to conquer her pas-

---

2 In the translation, I have rendered this word, and its cognates, as "moderation, moderate," "virtue, virtuous," "chastity, chaste," "sensible" depending on the context, but its full semantic range should be borne in mind.

sion by being *sophron* (399), hates those who are *sophron* only in words (413), and dies hoping that Hippolytus will learn to be *sophron* (731). From the Nurse's perspective, Phaedra is not *sophron* (358, 494), nor is she herself, she admits, in telling Hippolytus about Phaedra's passion (704), and, from Theseus' point of view, neither is Hippolytus (949). The chorus voices the commonplace that *sophrosune* is a good thing (431-2). The different claims about *sophrosune* and its varying shades of meaning conform with and help to create the ambiguities, paradoxes, and failures of understanding which permeate and animate the drama.

Hippolytus' assertion that he is *sophron* is matched by his assertion that he is *semnos*: "Here I am the reverent (*semnos*) and god-revering,/ here I am the one who surpassed everyone in *sophrosune*" (1364-5). But the word *semnos* is ambiguous and charged. It is used in both negative ("arrogant," "proud") and positive ("august," "revered," "pious") senses. In a telling scene with his servant, this word appears three times in shifting senses. This dialogue suggests that it is one thing for a god to be *semnos* (in its positive sense), another for a mortal to be *semnos* (in its negative sense) (88-105; see 93n.). Aphrodite has already made clear that Hippolytus will be punished for his refusal to reverence her. Hence his claim to being *semnos*, juxtaposed to the paradoxical claim of surpassing everyone in *sophrosune*, rings ominously.

PASSION AND REASON

Sexual passion, refused by Hippolytus and combated by Phaedra, drives the play's action, and much of the play can be read as a discourse on passion. Aphrodite faults Hippolytus for reviling her (12-3; and cf. 113) and also, strikingly, not for neglecting her altar but for refusing her realm, the realm of marriage and sex (14). But what she wants from him is impossible if he is going to continue as a virgin follower of Artemis. And this impossibility is the essence of his tragedy. Artemis explains the situation concisely: "She [Aphrodite] found fault with your homage, and she was vexed at your virtue" (1402). Hippolytus has no place in his world for sex. In his extraordinary response to the Nurse's proposition (616-68), his world has no place for women at all, and he even thinks he has been sullied by the Nurse's words (654-5). He consistently (and futilely) asserts his chastity and purity in his debate with his father (esp. 1003-6). For Phaedra, not passion *per se*, but an illicit passion for her stepson is at issue. This passion is imagined as a disease. The word *nosos* is used frequently both of the passion itself and of the effects it has on Phaedra. It is a sickness because it is illicit and too strong; it threatens the good name that is so important to her.

The Nurse, on the other hand, sees sexual passion, of whatever sort, simply as part of life, something sent from the Aphrodite (437-40) that afflicts the gods as well as mortals (451-61). When it leads to illicit acts, it is best to ignore them (462-9). She recognizes the important role Aphrodite plays throughout the universe (447-50) and even sees her as something greater than divinity (359-60). She argues that the one who opposes Aphrodite is struck that much harder by the goddess (443-6), and that it is even *hubris* to try to fight passion (473-6). Theseus, like the Nurse, responds to the effects of passion, but, unlike the Nurse, responds to a distorted version of those effects. He readily accepts Phaedra's version of what happened, not only because of the damning evidence of the corpse and the lying note, but because the false tale she created conforms to his belief about young men (966-70).

The choral songs, especially the first stasimon, contribute to the play's exploration of passion. The *parodos* ironically considers Theseus' infidelity as a possible cause of Phaedra's distress (151-4). The next choral song (525-64), sung after the revelation of Phaedra's desire for Hippolytus and while the Nurse approaches the young man within, offers the play's most extended reflection on passion. The chorus describe Eros as a warrior, yet, paradoxically, one who brings "sweet delight" to those he attacks, echoing the motif of Eros the bittersweet already introduced by the Nurse (348). These women of Trozen pray that this god not come to them with evil intent or "out of measure," recognizing that it is under such circumstances that Eros is intolerable. This prayer reflects the dynamics of the play: passion under "proper" circumstances is (implicitly) welcome and benign; otherwise it can be ruinous. The rest of the song focuses on the destructive power of desire, proclaiming the lack of ritual observance Eros receives and then recounting the specific examples of destructive passion in the cases of Zeus and Semele and Heracles and Iole. Permeating the second half of the song are terms and images associated with weddings, used so as to suggest the perversion of wedding rituals. Broadly the song points to the destructiveness of passion, which brings down, directly or indirectly, all three of the play's main characters. More specifically, it hints that the perversion of these rituals leads to these characters' ruin. Phaedra does not violate her marriage, but it is the fear that she might that leads her to her death. Hippolytus' violation of marital norms is in his extraordinary refusal to participate in them, announced by Aphrodite and obliquely echoed in this song's concern with the lack of observance paid to Eros. Theseus' "violation" of these norms is oblique. His sexual transgressions were notorious, but what draws attention in this play is the bastardy of Hippolytus. Repeatedly we are reminded that the unstable familial situation (a bastard child who poses a sexual temptation to Theseus' wife) stems from his sexual transgression. And, as already noted, his ready assumptions about a male's sexual behavior lead him to condemn his son precipitously.

Following Phaedra's exit to her death, the chorus wish to escape from their present plight and revert, in the second half of the song, to Phaedra's ill-omened wedding voyage from Crete to Athens. They connect this directly with her suffering and her current illicit passion, caused by Aphrodite, which is leading to her death. At Hippolytus' departure, the chorus lament the loss of Hippolytus, including the loss to maidens of a contest for his hand (1140-1). The invocation of the "yoked Graces" (1148) might evoke images of a wedding. The brief choral song preceding the *exodos* is devoted fully to the overwhelming force of passion, hymning the power of Eros and Aphrodite. Here, near the play's conclusion, the song emphasizes the universal, procreative, and overwhelming power of these gods or forces, rather than their destructiveness. In her final speech, Artemis establishes Hippolytus' paradoxical connection with marriage rites, promising that Trozenian maidens before their weddings will honor him in cult and will remember Phaedra's passion for him in song.

Passion has several forces opposing it in this play. Moderation and reason in particular are imagined in opposition to it (ultimately without success). *Sophrosune*, as discussed above, although frequently approximating English "virtue" or "moderation," literally refers to one's intellect ("safe-mindedness"). So even *sophrosune's* opposition to passion can be viewed as part of a larger opposition of reason and passion. Phaedra clearly imagines her struggle in terms of intellection. Words for intellection dominate the entire speech in which she explains her course of actions. She describes her struggle against her passion for Hippolytus in cerebral terms, concluding that, since she could not subjugate it, she must choose death. The chorus, as they conclude their song in response to her presumed death, describe it, using the same opposition, as Phaedra's attempt to rid this passion from her mind (774-5). Earlier Phaedra attributed her expressions of desire (198ff.) to madness and ruin (241), which led her away from the course of good thinking (240). And the Nurse, after recovering from her initial shock at the object of Phaedra's passion, tells her that she suffers nothing "unaccountable" (literally "beyond reason," 438). For Hippolytus there is no comparable internal conflict. His *sophrosune* brings about his ruin, and his power of speech, curtailed by his sworn oath, and his argumentation are unable to save him. Sexual passion overcomes him, but only indirectly. Theseus acts rashly, his powers of reflection and considered judgment overtaken by the anger induced by Phaedra's lying note (1310-2, 1336-7; and cf. 1413). In the play as a whole, speech is typically portrayed as destructive, while reason is shown to be unable to cope with the forces of passion.

IGNORANCE

Aphrodite's opening speech creates at once a fundamental dramatic irony—we know (more or less) what is going to transpire, while the play's characters do not. Such dramatic irony is not uncommon, especially in plays in which a god delivers the prologue, but ignorance, real and feigned, resonates throughout this play, in big ways and small. Aphrodite explains that none of the servants knows Phaedra's malady (40), and that Hippolytus does not know that the gates of Hades lie open for him (56-7). The servant introduces his exchange with Hippolytus with a question about his master's knowledge (91); the chorus's first words when the Nurse enters reflect their ignorance about Phaedra's condition (173-5; and cf. 270 and 282-3), and the Nurse herself is ignorant of the cause of Phaedra's illness (271), and shows her confusion in response to Phaedra's "delirium." The Nurse does evoke a response from a silent Phaedra when she mentions the name of Hippolytus, whom, she says, "you know well" (309), but only gradually does she learn what she wishes to know (see 344, 346). Phaedra's speech on knowledge and our limitations in carrying out the good forms another part of this matrix. The Nurse does not so much persuade Phaedra as dupe her, resorting to an evasive claim of ignorance about her own plans (517). When she learns Hippolytus' response to what the Nurse has actually done, Phaedra says, "I don't know, except one thing—to die as quickly as possible" (599). Hippolytus himself is ignorant of the full import of his oath to the Nurse. And this oath compels him to feign ignorance in the confrontation with his father (1033), after an initial honest claim of ignorance about the cause of Theseus' alarm (903-4). At the end of the scene with his father, he refers enigmatically to the constraints of this oath, "I know these things, but I don't know how to reveal them" (1091). The chorus's oath to Phaedra also constrains them to lie about their knowledge in response to Theseus' question about her death (804-5). Theseus laments that mortals do not yet know how to teach good sense (919-20); he does, however, claim to know how young men are affected by passion (967-70), a general statement which does not apply to his son. Hippolytus, in this debate with his father, asserts his knowledge of proper behavior (996ff.) and his ignorance of sex (1004-5), an ignorance that has ignited Aphrodite's wrath.

Because of the lying tablet and the sworn oaths, Theseus acts in the most profound and destructive ignorance. Yet this very ignorance acquits him, in Artemis' view, from the charge of wickedness (1334-5). Ignorance, as much as anything else, separates mortals from the gods and defines the human condition. Human characters make crucial choices—for speech, for silence, for vengeance—in ignorance. Phaedra claims that mortals know what is right but cannot carry it out. The play, however, strongly suggests that mortals too often do not know enough even to begin to make the right decisions, and do not seek out further information. Passion is an overwhelming force in mortals' lives, and so is ignorance. Both forces act on mortals to bring about the play's multiple acts of destruction.

Suggestions for Further Reading

The bibliography on Greek tragedy, the ancient theater, Euripides and the *Hippolytus* is enormous. The following is a selection of works that are informative and accessible.

THE THEATER AND PRODUCTION

Gould, J. "Tragedy in Performance," in *The Cambridge History of Classical Literature, Volume I: Greek Literature*, eds. P. E. Easterling, B. M. W. Knox (Cambridge 1985), 263-81

Green, J. R. and E. W. Handley *Images of the Greek Theatre* (London 1995)

Pickard-Cambridge, A. W. *The Theatre of Dionysus in Athens* (Oxford 1946)

Pickard-Cambridge, A. W. *The Dramatic Festivals of Athens*, 3rd edition by J. Gould and D. M. Lewis (Oxford 1990)

Rehm, R. *Greek Tragic Theatre* (London and New York, 1992)

Taplin, O. *Greek Tragedy in Action* (London 1978)

Wiles, D. *Tragedy in Athens: Performance Space and Theatrical Meaning* (Cambridge 1997)

EURIPIDES' LIFE AND SOCIETY

Cairns, D. *Aidos: The Psychology and Ethics of Honour and Shame in Ancient Greek Literature* (Oxford 1993)

Dodds, E. R. *The Greeks and the Irrational* (Berkeley and Los Angeles 1951)

Dover, K. J. *Greek Popular Morality in the Time of Plato and Aristotle* (Berkeley and Los Angeles 1974)

Ehrenberg, V. *From Solon to Socrates*, 2nd edition (London 1973)

Pomeroy, S., et al. *Ancient Greece: A Political, Social and Cultural History* (Oxford 1999)

Stevens, P. T. "Euripides and the Athenians," *Journal of Hellenic Studies* 76 (1976), 76-84

Williams, B. *Shame and Necessity* (Berkeley and Los Angeles 1993)

The World of Athens: An Introduction to Classical Culture (Cambridge 1984)

GENERAL WORKS ON EURIPIDES AND GREEK TRAGEDY
(THOSE MARKED WITH AN ASTERISK INCLUDE A STUDY OF THE *HIPPOLYTUS*)

Burnett, A. P. *Catastrophe Survived: Euripides' Plays of Mixed Reversal* (Oxford 1971)

Collard, C. *Euripides*, 'Greece and Rome' New Surveys in the Classics, No. 14 (Oxford 1981)

Conacher, D. J. *Euripidean Drama : Myth, Theme and Structure* (Toronto 1967)*

Easterling, P. E., ed. *The Cambridge Companion to Greek Tragedy* (Cambridge 1997)

Foley, H. P. *Ritual Irony. Poetry and Sacrifice in Euripides* (Cornell 1985)

Goldhill, S. *Reading Greek Tragedy* (Cambridge 1986)*

Gregory, J. *Euripides and the Instruction of the Athenians* (Ann Arbor 1991)*

Halleran, M. *Stagecraft in Euripides* (London 1985)

Jones, J. *On Aristotle and Greek Tragedy* (London 1962)

Lesky, A. *Greek Tragic Poetry*, trans. M. Dillon (New Have 1983)*

Michelini, A. N. *Euripides and the Tragic Tradition* (Wisconsin 1987)

Padel, R. *In and Out of the Mind: Greek Images of the Tragic Self* (Princeton 1992)

Seaford, R. A. *Reciprocity and Ritual: Homer and Tragedy in the Developing City State* (Oxford 1994)

Winkler, J. J. and F. I. Zeitlin, eds. *Nothing to do with Dionysos? Athenian Drama in its Social Context* (Princeton 1990)

Wohl, V. *Intimate Commerce: Exchange, Gender and Subjectivity in Greek Tragedy* (Austin 1998)

STUDIES OF THE *HIPPOLYTUS*

Craik, E. "AIDOS: *Hippolytos* 373-430: Review and Interpretation," *Journal of Hellenic Studies* 113 (1993), 45-59

Dunn, F. "Fearful Symmetry: the Two Tombs of *Hippolytus*," *Materiali e discussioni* 28 (1992), 103-11

Gill, C. "The Articulation of the Self in Euripides' *Hippolytus*," in A. Powell, ed., *Euripides, Women and Sexuality* (London 1990), 76-107

Goff, B. *The Noose of Words: Readings of Desire, Violence & Language in Euripides' Hippolytus* (Cambridge 1990)

Halleran, M. "*Gamos* and Destruction in Euripides' *Hippolytus*," *Transactions of the American Philological Association* 121 (1991), 109-21

Knox, B. M. W. "The *Hippolytus* of Euripides" in *Word and Action* (Baltimore 1979)

Kovacs, D. *The Heroic Muse* (Baltimore and London 1987)

Luschnig, C. *Time Holds a Mirror: A Study of Knowledge in Euripides' Hippolytus. Mnemosyne* Supplement 102 (Leiden 1988)

Reckford, K. "Phaedra and Pasiphaë: The Pull Backwards," *Transactions of the American Philological Association* 104 (1974), 307-28

Segal, C. P. *Interpreting Greek Tragedy: Myth, Poetry, Text* (Ithaca 1986)

Zeitlin, F. "The Power of Aphrodite: Eros and the Boundaries of the Self in the *Hippolytus*," in *Playing the Other: Gender and Society in Classical Greek Literature* (Chicago 1996), 341-74